Meals and Memories:
How To Create Keepsake Cookbooks

Kathy Steligo

Published by Carlo Press, PO Box 7080, San Carlos, CA 94070-7080
        Website: www.carlopress.com/books
        e-mail: carlop@pacbell.net

This publication is designed to provide accurate information in regard to the subject matter covered. It is sold with the understanding that the publisher is not engaged in rendering legal or other professional services. If legal advice or other expert assistance is required, the services of a competent professional person should be sought.

Cover: Graphic images courtesy of Dogbyte Development, Inc.

Publisher's Cataloging in Publication Data:

Steligo, Kathy
        Meals and memories : how to create keepsake cookbooks / Kathy Steligo.
        112 p. : ill. ; 27.94 cm.
        Includes index.
        ISBN 0-9669799-0-7 (pbk.)
        1. Scrapbooks — Design and construction. 2. Souvenirs (Keepsakes)
        3. Cookery — Authorship.
     745.59--dc21   99-90018

PRINTED IN THE USA

10 9 8 7 6 5 4 3 2 1

To Charles

For the very best memories and those yet to come

Table of Contents

"There is no sincerer love than the love of food."— George Bernard Shaw

INTRODUCTION

Food is something we all have in common. Everyone eats to live (although some of us like to think we live to eat). In its endless forms, food delights, comforts, and sustains us. Whether simple fare or regal repast, food is a member of the family—an integral part of our daily routines and special occasions. When we document recipes for these foods, and add related stories and memories, we preserve an important connection between past and future generations—our culinary heritage. All too often, we omit this elemental piece of history from the family album. Our unique foods and related traditions may grow dimmer and dimmer with each generation until they fade away, simply because we failed to record them.

Why not create a keepsake cookbook to preserve your own culinary history? Whether simple or elaborate, your cookbook can impart a sense of tradition to your children in a way no commercial cookbook can equal. Your children will thank you. And, hopefully, they will carry on the tradition; adding new recipes as they establish new traditions, and passing them along to their children. You'll find many other reasons to create a keepsake cookbook: organize your own recipes, make a unique gift for a friend, remember a special vacation, or develop a profitable fundraiser. But be forewarned, creating keepsake cookbooks becomes addicting. You'll make one, then another, then another...

Kathy Steligo

Recipe for a Keepsake Cookbook
- Start with a generous helping of your favorite recipes
- Spice with memories, anecdotes, and stories
- Fold in photos, drawings, or doodles
- Pepper with dashes of humor and nostalgia to taste
- Combine all and blend well
- Serve up to yourself, family, and friends

STARTING WITH THE BASICS

"When we prepare dishes handed down to us from our grandmothers, we become grandchildren again, reconnected to the people who have gone before us. When we prepare traditional food for our children, we give them memories they can turn to when they are grown and cut adrift. They will prepare these foods and once again be grounded with their families in time."
—*Judith Comfort's Christmas Cookbook* (1988)

1. BEFORE YOU BEGIN

In This Chapter:

- What's a Keepsake?
- How This Book is Organized
- Handwritten or High-tech?
- Mind Your Copyright Manners
- A Caution About Acid

What's a Keepsake?

A keepsake is an object of any size, color, or shape that is kept as a memento. It's something that instantly summons the warm fuzzy feeling of a happy memory: your baby's first shoes, your grandfather's gold watch, or a shell you found on the beach while on your honeymoon. Or a cookbook.

A keepsake cookbook is more than just a set of recipes. It's a personalized collection of favorite recipes and special memories about them. All too often, we pass these recipes and memories from one generation to the next by word of mouth—a process that is well-meaning, but often loses more and more detail with each successive generation. When these family classics are not recorded, they can be lost altogether. A keepsake cookbook creates a lasting record of your culinary traditions that can be passed from one generation to the next. Like a ripe cheese or a fine wine, the family cookbook improves with age as each successive generation adds its own new recipes and traditions. How wonderful it would be if every child inherited a family cookbook. How many recipes and stories have gone unrecorded in your family already?

A keepsake cookbook is also an excellent way to document your family's new culinary traditions. Start your own keepsake and add to it as your family develops its own favorite recipes and memories. Or create a keepsake as a gift for someone special. These personalized cookbooks say "thank you," "congratulations," or "happy birthday" in a unique and creative fashion. A keepsake cookbook is something special you can develop to encourage and teach children to cook, or to give them as they leave home and have to cook for themselves.

Don't forget to treat yourself to a keepsake: record the recipes and memories of a fabulous vacation, a special occasion, or organize all the recipes you've collected over the years into one or more cookbooks.

A keepsake cookbook is a personalized collection of recipes. It may also include related stories, memories, photos, and illustrations.

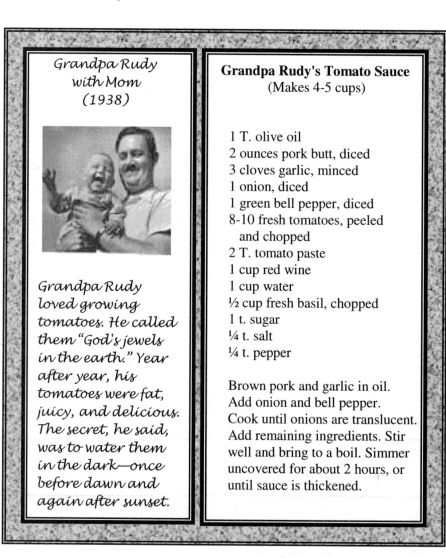

Grandpa Rudy with Mom (1938)

Grandpa Rudy loved growing tomatoes. He called them "God's jewels in the earth." Year after year, his tomatoes were fat, juicy, and delicious. The secret, he said, was to water them in the dark—once before dawn and again after sunset.

Grandpa Rudy's Tomato Sauce
(Makes 4-5 cups)

1 T. olive oil
2 ounces pork butt, diced
3 cloves garlic, minced
1 onion, diced
1 green bell pepper, diced
8-10 fresh tomatoes, peeled
    and chopped
2 T. tomato paste
1 cup red wine
1 cup water
½ cup fresh basil, chopped
1 t. sugar
¼ t. salt
¼ t. pepper

Brown pork and garlic in oil.
Add onion and bell pepper.
Cook until onions are translucent.
Add remaining ingredients. Stir well and bring to a boil. Simmer uncovered for about 2 hours, or until sauce is thickened.

How This Book is Organized

This book is a guide for planning, organizing, and assembling your keepsake cookbook. Each chapter explains what to do and how to do it, then summarizes with a step-by-step checklist. These checklists will help guide you whether you're creating a very simple or very elaborate cookbook. As you complete successive chapters, your keepsake cookbook will begin to take shape. Here's a preview:

<u>Sections</u>	<u>Chapters</u>
Starting with the Basics:	1. Before You Begin (this chapter) 2. Cookbook Fundamentals
Planning Your Keepsake:	3. Pick a Theme, Tone, and Title 4. Design the Look of Your Cookbook
Collecting and Organizing Your Materials:	5. Collect Recipes 6. Format Recipes 7. Record Your Memories 8. Add Photos, Illustrations, and Other Images
Putting It All Together:	9. Create Your Pages 10. Add Finishing Touches and Assemble Your Cookbook
More Ideas:	11. Cookbooks As Profitable Fundraisers 12. 101 Themes for Keepsake Cookbooks
Appendix:	This section includes a master checklist of the steps in Chapters 3 through 10, a list of the resources mentioned throughout the book, and other information you can include in your own cookbooks.

You'll find plenty of examples, tips, and illustrations. Throughout the text, these icons indicate special information:

Tips 'n Tools
Indicates special hints, tips, and sources for additional information. The products and suppliers listed are also summarized in the appendix.

Do It Yourself
Summarizes the information from each chapter into a checklist of steps to help you to progressively build your own keepsake cookbook.

Handwritten or High-tech?

The information in this book will be helpful whether you use a pen, a typewriter, or a computer to develop your keepsake. While a handwritten cookbook can be charming, your recipes and stories will be easier to read and will fit better on the page if they are typed. Here are some additional advantages of using a computer:

- Duplicates standard recipe formats and page layouts in a snap.

- Makes it easy to make changes (you never need to erase).

- Adds a professional look to your cookbook.

- Provides access to hundreds of lettering styles, sizes, and designs.

- Maintains an expanding archive of recipes that can be easily updated and reproduced (just print out another copy) without creating a huge demand for storage.

- Places additional desktop publishing capabilities squarely onto your desktop by use of peripheral devices like scanners, CD-ROMs, and color printers.

- Provides access via disks, CDs, and the Internet to thousands of recipes, fonts, clip art, photographs, cartoons, quotations, and other potential materials for your cookbook.

One way to combine the two methods is to type most of your text, and limit your handwriting to short stories or notes about the recipes. You might even include a handwritten shopping list for a recipe's ingredients.

Tips 'n Tools
The Cook's Palate by Better Lifestyles, Inc. is computer software specifically designed to organize recipe collections and create cookbooks. It includes a large database of recipes (you can also add your own), nutritional analysis of ingredients, shopping lists, menu plans, and many other interactive features. Contact: (800) 278-5136. On the Internet: http://www.cookspalate.com.

Mind Your Copyright Manners

As you collect materials for your keepsake, you may come across a poem, song lyric, or cartoon that perfectly conveys your sentiment. If these materials are protected by a copyright, you may use them without permission for personal use only (yours or someone else's). If you intend to sell your keepsake for profit (a fundraiser, for example), you must always obtain the author's permission before using copyrighted materials. In either case, always credit the author.

A Caution About Acid

Have you ever seen albums of photos that are faded, yellowed, or brittle? That's because the albums are made with vinyl, PVC, or other plastics containing acid. Over time, the acid migrates to the photos, causing the deterioration. Inexpensive photo albums with magnetic overlays are especially guilty of acid damage. To avoid this problem, choose albums and materials that are labeled acid-free. This certifies that the album contains materials that will not harm your photographs. Be suspicious of a photo-safe label—it's not the same as acid-free. A photo-safe label on an album is akin to "healthy" label on foods: broadly defined and highly suspect.

It's also a good idea to use papers, pens, adhesives, and other materials that are labeled acid-free. These are now widely available in many stores that sell scrapbook, photo, and office supplies.

You can create a keepsake cookbook to record recipes and related memories from a special event or occasion.

Preserve your favorite childhood recipes and the special memories you have about them.

Whenever these sandwiches appeared in my school lunch bag, I swapped with my classmates for their cheese and mayonnaise on white bread.

My pals loved the eggplant on thick slabs of Mom's homemade bread, while I liked the greasy stuff we never got at home.

Now, my tastes have changed; I wouldn't trade these for anything!

Eggplant Sandwiches (Makes 4)

2 T. olive oil
1 medium eggplant, halved lengthwise
2 tomatoes, peeled, seeded, and diced
2 T. Parmesan cheese, shredded or sliced
½ t. dried basil
½ t. dried oregano
Salt and pepper to taste
8 slices whole wheat or sourdough bread

Preheat oven to 375°. Heat oil in large skillet until hot. Add eggplant, cut sides down. Reduce heat to medium and cook until golden (about 5-7 minutes). Turn eggplant and cook other sides. Remove from pan and arrange in a 2-quart baking dish. Top with tomatoes, cheese, basil, oregano, salt, and pepper. Cover and bake 30-35 minutes until eggplant is tender. Remove from oven. When cooled, slice eggplant and place between slices of bread.

"We may live without poetry, music and art.
We may live without conscience and live without heart.
We may live without friends,
We may live without books,
But civilized man cannot live without cooks."
—Greek writer Athenaeus

2. COOKBOOK FUNDAMENTALS

In This Chapter

- The Four Basics
- Additional Parts to Mix and Match
- Do It Yourself

Before you begin collecting recipes, jotting down memories, and sorting through photos, it's a good idea to understand a few cookbook fundamentals. This chapter discusses common cookbook parts that should always be included in your keepsakes: the front and back covers, the table of contents, and, of course, the recipes. It also describes other parts you might want to include as well.

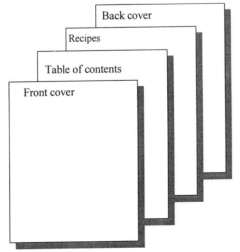

The Four Basics

Front and Back Covers. The front and back covers protect the contents of your keepsake. Both covers should be sturdy enough to withstand handling and use. Because the front cover will be handled every time the book is opened, and the back cover may come in contact with damp counters and tabletops, paper covers are a poor choice. They tear easily, absorb dampness, and can't be expected to hold up to frequent handling.

Create a cover with a simply-stated title (left) or a sense of humor (right).

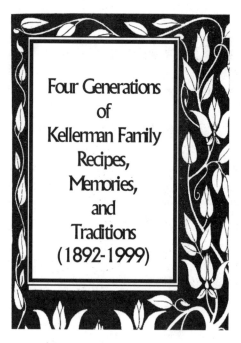

You can also incorporate a drawing or photograph into your cover.

Table of Contents. The table of contents is a roadmap to the rest of your cookbook. It helps you organize the contents and helps the reader to quickly find recipes. Here are several different formats to consider:

- **Alphabetical.** List your recipes alphabetically: Apple Pie, Boysenberry Crisp, Cherry Cobbler, Chocolate Cream Pie, etc. Or, list the types of recipes alphabetically: Cobblers, Cream Pies, Crisps, Fruit Pies, Tarts, etc.

- **Meal Type.** Organize recipes by the kind of meal: Breakfast, Lunch, Brunch, Dinner, Snacks, etc.

- **Sequential.** Lists courses in the order they are normally served: Appetizers/Hors d'oeuvres, Soups, Salads, Breads, Pasta, Meat and Poultry, Vegetables, Fruits, Desserts.

- **Seasonal.** This is a logical format for any recipes that celebrate seasonal ingredients or activities. Organize recipes according to the seasons of the year (Spring, Summer, Autumn, and Winter), or seasons specific to the type of recipes you're including. For example, holiday recipes might be listed chronologically as Valentine's Day, Easter, Fourth of July, Halloween, Thanksgiving, and Christmas.

- **Special Dietary Interests.** List recipes by nutritional content: Less than 500 calories, Low-fat, Nonfat, High fiber, Reduced sodium, Low cholesterol, etc.

- **Technique.** Use this format to organize recipes according to:

  a. Method of preparation: Blender, Bread Machine, Microwave, Oven, Stovetop, etc.

  b. Skill level required: Beginner, Intermediate, or Advanced. Always write to the skill level of the intended reader.

  c. Time required to prepare each recipe. You might group these recipes in different categories, including all those which can be prepared in 30 minutes or less, those which take more than an hour, and so on.

When you develop your table of contents, decide how much detail you want to show. You may decide to simply reflect the organization of your cookbook, or provide more detail by listing the recipes within each section. More detail makes it easier to find a specific recipe, especially if you don't have an index. Look at the table of contents in different cookbooks to see which format you find most appealing. Set your table of contents against a plain background, or be creative and include a design that compliments your overall theme. The following two examples show different levels of detail for a keepsake cookbook of seasonal recipes.

Create a table of contents that simply reflects the organization of your cookbook.

The Bailey Family's

Four Seasons Cookbook

Spring Recipes........................3

Summer Recipes....................11

Autumn Recipes....................16

Winter Recipes......................23

Show more detail by listing all the recipes within each section.

The Bailey Family's

Four Seasons Cookbook

Spring_____ 3
Barbeque Lamb Kabobs • Grilled Salmon
Filet with Caper Sauce • Tomato & Maui
Onion Salad • Cherry Meringues • Straw-
berry Shortcake

Summer_____ 11
Asparagus, Fig, & Prosciutto Appetizer
• Grilled Chicken and Peach Halves
• Roast Pepper & Onion Fajitas • Herb
Garlic Bread • Green Apple Cobbler
• Vanilla Ice Cream

Autumn_____ 16
Stuffed Pork Tenderloin • Garlic Mashed
Potatoes • Yam Soup • Corn Fritters
• Spinach, Walnut, & Feta Salad • Late
Harvest Herb Marinade

Winter_____ 23
Baked Whole Chicken • Lentil Soup
• Swordfish with Sun-dried Tomatoes
• Porcini Mushroom Cabernet Sauce
• Devil's Food Cookies • Orange Sorbet

Tips 'n Tools
Many computer word processing applications will automatically create and revise your table of contents. For more information, check the User Guide or Help menu for your application.

The Recipes. Recipes are the main attraction in your cookbook. Show them on a page by themselves, add brief introductions or cooking tips, or include small photos or drawings.

▶   Chapters 5 and 6 explain everything you need to know about including recipes in your keepsake.

Additional Parts to Mix and Match

In addition to the front and back covers, table of contents, and recipes, you can add other parts to your cookbook to add interest or improve organization. The shaded pages below show these optional parts: the title and dedication pages, section pages, memories and photos that accompany your recipes, the appendix, and the index.

Note: The single section of recipes shown below is for illustrative purposes only. Organize your keepsake recipes into as many sections as you think necessary.

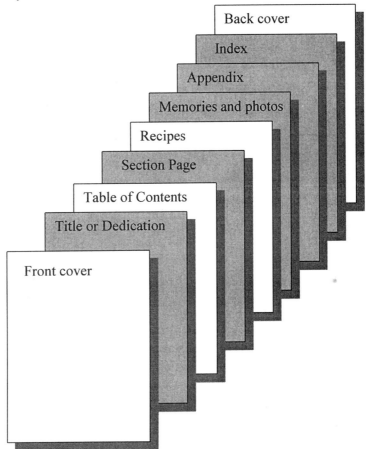

Tips 'n Tools
Look through cookbooks to see first-hand how these optional pages are presented. Notice what you like and what you don't, then decide for yourself which parts you want to include in your cookbook.

Title or Dedication Page. Commercial cookbooks usually include a title page and a dedication page. You can do the same in your keepsake. Combine the title with any acknowledgment, dedication, or introduction you want to include.

If you design a cover page for the front of your cookbook, you can use a title page as an introduction or a dedication.

Created Especially for Polly Samson

The Seafood Cookbook

Thanks for 12 years of fun and friendship. With Love,
Jonathan & Susan Farewell

If you don't create a cover page for the front of your cookbook (perhaps your album has a fabric or pre-designed cover), create a title page for the inside instead.

Through Feast and Famine:

Tales and Lessons from Paddy O'Brien's Kitchen

Adapt a title or dedication page to suit the purpose of your keepsake. This dedication page from one family's cookbook acknowledges all past, present, and future family members.

Thank you to our ancestors for the foods and customs that have become Rinaldi family traditions.

Thank you to current family members for your research, input, and interest in helping to create this living record of our family's culinary history.

Thank you to future family members for carrying on these traditions and creating new ones.

John, Stacey, and Rose Rinaldi
San Antonio, Texas
April 1998

Section Pages. You can use a section page to introduce each different category of recipes (think of a section page as a table of contents or title page for each category). Make these pages as simple or elaborate as you wish. List the section title simply or use quotations, anecdotes, photos, or illustrations. Add tabs or use paper of different weight or color to distinguish section pages from the rest of your cookbook.

Use section pages to list the recipes within each category.

AUTUMN RECIPES

- ▶ Stuffed Pork Tenderloin
- ▶ Garlic Mashed Potatoes
- ▶ Yam Soup
- ▶ Corn Fritters
- ▶ Spinach, Walnut, and Feta Salad
- ▶ Late Harvest Herb Marinade

A section page can also deliver a personal message. If several people are contributing to your cookbook, this is a handy way for contributors to introduce their own recipe sections.

Dear Hank & Kate,

You always said you'd love to have the recipes for my apple, yam, plum, and sweet potato pies. Here they are! I'm happy to share my "secrets" with you both.

I hope you take as much delight in making and eating them as I do.

Enjoy!
Virginia Roberts

Appendix. The appendix follows the body of recipes. Include any interesting or helpful information not associated with specific recipes. Examples might include menu plans, shopping lists, nutritional information, lists of ingredient substitutes, or a glossary of terms.

▶   See the Appendix of this book for examples of some of these additional materials.

Index. Most commercial cookbooks include an index of all the recipe titles and major recipe ingredients. Decide early in your project whether you consider an index as overkill or want to include one in your keepsake. If you decide to add an index, it's easier to compile items as you proceed rather than backtrack through your entire cookbook looking for index items. Notice how index items are listed in the cookbooks you most prefer. Think about how you want to list items in your index before you begin putting your pages together.

Many word processing applications also have automatic indexing features. Check the User Guide or Help menu for information specific to your application.

▶   Chapters 9 and 10 explain how to create an index.

Do It Yourself

❏ Decide how you want to format your table of contents, and how much detail you want to include.

❏ Determine which optional cookbook parts, if any, you want to include.

❏ Decide whether you want to build an index. If you do, determine which items you want to list.

You'll actually create your table of contents and optional cookbook parts in Chapters 9 and 10.

Next step: Pick a Theme, Tone, and Title.

PLANNING YOUR KEEPSAKE

"Older people often leave property or money behind for their descendants, but a package of memories of a person's life is what usually doesn't get passed along. The most precious commodities of all—people's own recollections of their worlds—seldom get preserved."
—Bob Greene, *To Our Children's Children*

3. PICK A THEME, TONE, AND TITLE

In This Chapter:

- Start with a Theme
- Set the Tone
- Your Title: Tell It Like It Is
- Do It Yourself

Start with a Theme

The first step in building your keepsake cookbook is deciding on an overall theme. It becomes the common thread that connects all your recipes, memories, and photos. The theme for a family keepsake, for example, might reflect historical or contemporary culinary traditions. If you're creating a keepsake to give as a gift, consider the lucky recipient. What is she passionate about? What hobbies does he pursue? What collection of recipes would absolutely delight her?

Keeping your theme in mind as you plan, organize, and asemble your materials helps you to stay on track and visualize the final version of your cookbook. If your theme is your family's Lithuanian recipes and related traditions, you probably won't include a recipe for strawberry shortcake (unless it happens to be a family favorite or specialty). That shortcake recipe, however, will fit right in with a cookbook of recipes for summer fruits or desserts.

▶ See Chapter 12 for 101 theme ideas.

Set the Tone

The theme is *what* your cookbook is all about; the tone is *how* you convey that theme through the recipes, memories, photos, and illustrations. Do you want your keepsake to give a sense of nostalgia, whimsy, romance, serenity, or fun? Will your cookbook be sweet and sassy, bright and classy, or bold and brassy? Keep your theme and tone in mind as you collect recipes, record your memories, select photos, or create illustrations.

Suppose you plan to make a keepsake cookbook for your daughter, who will soon be a mother herself. You plan to include recipes for all her favorite childhood foods. To emphasize a nostalgic tone, accompany the recipes with your memories of holding and feeding your daughter for the first time, and the first time she helped you in the kitchen. Then add a few of her childhood photos or drawings. For a more whimsical tone, choose photos of her making a face or standing on her head. Then add anecdotes in big, chunky cartoon letters. Describe the funny face she made when she first tried stewed prunes, how she liked to eat peas with her fingers, or the time she shared her ice cream with the dog.

Your Title: Tell It Like It Is

Choose a title that is consistent with your theme and tone, and clearly tells what your cookbook is about. Don't be surprised if a title eludes you at first. The perfect title might not reveal itself until you're well into the develpment of your cookbook. Look through poetry, song lyrics, quotations, and greeting cards for inspriation. If all else fails, something will come to mind when you begin creating and assembling all your cookbook materials.

Do It Yourself

☐ Select a theme for your keepsake.

☐ Decide on the tone or mood you want to convey.

☐ Draft five or six titles for the theme and tone you've chosen. Set them aside for a few days. Then choose the title you most prefer, making any changes you think necessary.

Next step: Design the look of your cookbook.

"Tell me what you eat and I will tell you who you are."—Athelme Brillat-Savrin

4. DESIGN THE LOOK OF YOUR COOKBOOK

In This Chapter:

* Select a Page Format
* Try a Few Fancy Fonts
* Find the Perfect Album
* Planning for Multiple Copies
* Pick Your Pages, Fill Your Pockets
* Do It Yourself

In this chapter, you'll decide how you want your keepsake to look, both inside and out. You'll decide how you want to format the information on your cookbook pages, consider all the possibilities for albums or binders, and decide what type of pages you prefer.

Select a Page Format

The first step in designing your cookbook is to plan the look of your pages. Using a consistent page layout throughout your cookbook will give it a clean, uniform appearance. Whether you create a very simple or very elaborate cookbook, there are two basic ways to format your pages: you either create a one-page format or a two-page format. In the one-page format, the information on each page is unrelated to other pages. A two-page format displays related information across facing pages. Within each format, there are many ways to position your recipes, memories, and photos. The following examples show how to use these formats in different ways to display your cookbook materials. Other examples throughout this book also use these same basic formats in different ways. Use one of these examples for your page format, select a format from a favorite cookbook, or design your own.

Note: You can also display your pages horizontally (not shown in examples).

One-page format. In this format the information on each page is unrelated.

For a simple but effective cookbook, display a different recipe on each page. You can also add a brief memory or anecdote (right), or a small photo, illustration, or other image to some or all of your recipes.

Garden Vegetable Soup
(Makes 8 cups)

Combine and bring to a boil:

6 cups chicken or beef stock
½ cup celery, sliced
½ cup carrot, peeled and diced
½ cup onion, diced
1 cup potato, diced
½ cup corn kernels
½ cup lima or other beans
2 cloves garlic, minced
4 t. tomato paste

Simmer 15-20 minutes. Add
¼ cup chopped fresh basil
and salt and pepper to taste.

Southwestern Pizza
(Makes 8 slices)

1 prepared pizza crust
½ cup shredded cheddar cheese
1 16-oz. can black beans, rinsed
   and drained
1 6-oz. can sliced black olives
2 green onions, sliced thinly
Hot sauce to taste

Preheat oven to 450°. In the order listed, spread ingredients evenly over crust. Bake for 10-15 minutes or until crust is browned and cheese is melted. Remove from oven and slice into eight pieces. Serve immediately.

Mom made this pizza for Rob's 8th birthday, when his party had a western theme. Now it's a family favorite.

In this one-page format, recipes are shown on both pages, with other text and images in the outer margins.

BABY'S APPLESAUCE

Use ripe apples that are not too tart:

-Fuji
-Gala
-Golden
 Delicious
-Macintosh

5 or 6 medium apples
½ cup unsweetened
   apple juice or water

Peel and quarter apples. Put in medium saucepan with juice. Simmer uncovered over low heat until apples are soft. Purée until smooth. Cover and refrigerate for up to a week or freeze.

JAKE'S BABY 'BAMAS

1 ripe banana, peeled
3 T. apple juice

Combine banana and juice in a blender or food processor. Mix well. Or, mash banana with a fork and mix in juice.

Yield: ½ cup

Jake says:

I like these 'bamas either warmed or at room temperature.

If warmed, always test temperature before serving Baby.

Choose a page format that works well for your theme. This one-page format, for example, is from a cookbook by four children for their grandma.

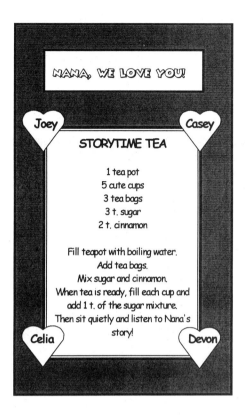

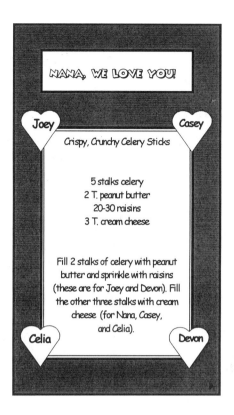

Two-Page Format. In this format, the recipe is shown on one page, with related information shown on the facing page.

The two-page format is handy for showing related recipes.

Chicken Broth

Place 3-4 lbs. chicken parts in a large soup pan or kettle. Add 1 onion, quartered; 1 carrot, cut into chunks; 1 stalk celery, chopped; ¼ c. chopped parsley; 1 bay leaf; and 8 cups water. Bring to boil over high heat. Then reduce heat and simmer, partially covered, for 2-3 hours. Strain mixture and skim off fat. Add salt and pepper to taste. Discard vegetables, bay leaf, and bones. Dice chicken meat, being careful to remove any bones. If made ahead, cool, cover, and refrigerate for up to 3 days or freeze. Store diced meat in a separate container.

Makes 2 quarts.

Recipe from:
Aunt Edna

Chicken Rice Soup

Bring 1 quart chicken broth to boil. Add 2 cups diced vegetables (use any combination of carrots, celery, onions, and potatoes). Stir in ½ cup rice, ¼ cup chopped fresh parsley, and 1 t. dried basil. Simmer, uncovered, until vegetables and rice are tender, about 15-20 minutes. Add salt and pepper to taste.

Makes 1½ quarts.

With a two-page format, you spread your cookbook materials across facing pages. This example uses stationary as a background.

Out on the river, there's no early, no late.
Just you and the fish, the sky, and the bait.
With white water swirling up to your hips,
Later with luck, there'll be trout on your lips.
And then a strike! His fight starts the game.
You twist, bend, and arch as he does the same.
His passion inspires you, gives you a thrill.
Except for you two, the world has gone still.
He pulls and leaps and crests into the air.
You're in this together; now you're a pair.
As you reel him in, you admire his fight.
Then you release him—it's burgers tonight.

© Kathy Steligo

Dad's Campfire Trout
(Makes 6 servings)

6 fresh rainbow or other trout, cleaned
3 lemons
Dash salt
Whole springs of parsley, oregano, and
   basil

Squeeze juice of ½ lemon into cavity of
each trout, then pack herbs into cavities.
Sprinkle each fish with salt and wrap in foil.
Cook over coals for 5-6 minutes on each
side, or grill for 8-10 minutes on each side.
Serve immediately.

Using a two-page format, you can create a scrapbook page opposite the recipe.

"Waitin' for the big one"   It rained every day during
                             our '96 trip to Lake Otto.

I always looked forward to my annual fishing trips with Dad. After a dinner of fried trout, we'd sit around the campfire together and watch for shooting stars. Every time I fry up a pan of trout with Dan Jr., I remember those times with Dad.
—Daniel Shutes 8/95

"There's a fine line between fishing and
just standing on the shore like an
idiot!"—Dad (June 1973)

Dad's Campfire Trout
(Makes 6 servings)

6 fresh rainbow or other trout, cleaned
3 lemons
Dash salt
Whole springs of parsley, oregano,
   and basil

Squeeze juice of half a lemon into
cavity of each trout, then pack herbs
into cavities. Sprinkle each fish with
salt. Wrap trout separately in foil. Cook
over coals for 5-6 minutes on each side,
or on an open grill for 8-10 minutes on
each side. Serve immediately.

▶   The previous examples show how you can format your pages. Chapter 6 explains how to format recipes.

Try a Few Fancy Fonts

To pack some pizzazz into your pages, handletter or type a title that emphasizes a particular recipe or the overall theme and tone of your cookbook. Be selective and treat fancy fonts like powerful spices: a little goes a long way. Too little may be unnoticeable, too much may be overpowering, but just the right amount will give your pages a visual zing.

If you're using a computer, it's easy to create bold titles and decorative lettering. Check your word processing application to apply boldface, underlining, or italics to your text. Or use a font style that emphasizes your recipe or theme, as shown in the examples throughout this book.

Don't be afraid to try your hand at creative lettering. Try combining handwritten titles with typed recipes. Or put together quick and colorful titles with alphabet stickers.

Tips 'n Tools

If you're going to include any handwritten entries in your cookbook, consider reading one of these helpful books before you start putting pen to page.

ABC's of Creative Lettering by lettering expert Lindsay Ostrom. This award-winning guide has lettering examples for the beginner as well as the accomplished letterer. Contact: (916) 482-2288. On the Internet: www.scrapramento.com.

Alphabet Soup is a series of booklets by Wasatch Mt. Design. Try your hand at duplicating the letters or simply trace them. Contact: (801) 969-1808.

The Best of Creative Lettering is available from *Creating Keepsakes* scrapbooking magazine. The CD-ROM includes 12 fonts and over 100 lettering graphics. Contact: (888) 247-5282. On the Internet: www.creatingscrapbooks.com.

Find the Perfect Album

Would you pour your delicious pie filling into a soggy crust or layer your favorite sandwich ingredients between stale bread? Be just as careful when choosing the covers for your keepsakes, because they protect your recipes and memories within. Contemporary photo and scrapbook albums are ideal for keepsake cookbooks. You can also use three-ring binders and, for handwritten keepsakes, you can even use journals. If cost is an issue (with a fundraising cookbook, for example), you can have your cover copied onto cardstock and bound by a printer or copy service. Select an album or binder that not only looks good but also has these qualities:

- Durable, acid-free materials.

- A cover design that compliments your theme and tone, or has a pocket in which you can insert your own cover page.

- Meets other criteria you may have (the ability to lie flat or add pages, for example).

A smorgasbord of albums and binders can be used for keepsake cookbooks. Look in stores or catalogs that sell photo supplies, stationary, or scrapbook supplies.

Photo and scrapbook albums. The best quality albums available are made for photos and scrapbooking. You'll find mini-, standard-, and over-sized albums in every imaginable color and design. Some have covers of printed paper, fabric, leather, foil, or tapestry. These albums are available with a variety of bindings, including three-ring, screw-post, and spiral.

Binders. Three- or four-ring office-quality binders are inexpensive and are available in several colors. Because they're usually made of vinyl, you'll need acid-free page protectors to keep your photos safe.

Journals. Personal-size journals come in different shapes, colors, and designs, and many have acid-free pages. Although they are not designed to be used as cookbooks (they don't lie flat), the artsy, theme-oriented nature of these little books make them good choices for handwritten keepsakes, especially as gifts. Journals have sewn-in pages with or without lines. Some also feature quotations or small-scale artwork around a central theme. Using a journal for your cookbook leaves no room for error. The bound sheets eliminate the opportunity to redo or rearrange your pages, so careful planning is a must. You'll need to collect and carefully organize all your materials *before* you begin entering them onto the journal pages.

Journals can be used effectively for small, handwritten keepsakes. These small personalized cookbooks make thoughtful gifts.

From 1954-1959, we lived in the middle of an apple orchard. At harvest time, Mom gave us burlap bags to gather all the fallen apples we could carry. Michael and I always rode with Dad to the cider press, where, for just ten cents a gallon, the apples were transformed into tangy sweet cider. Dad always added raisins and sugar to a gallon or two of "grown-up cider," and stored them under the porch to ferment.

Apple Cider Syrup
(Makes about 1/2 cup)

1 cup apple cider
2 T. corn syrup
1 T. brown sugar
1 T. fresh lemon juice

Add all ingredients together in a small saucepan. Simmer, stirring occasionally, until the syrup is reduced by half (about 15-20 minutes). Use warm or at room temperature. Store in refrigerator.

Tips 'n Tools
If you can't find just the right album in a photo or scrapbook store, try one of the following sources for quality acid-free albums:

Century Photo Products has a good selection, including an "easel" album designed to stand on its own. You can also request personalized covers and spines. Contact: (800) 767-0777.
On the Internet: http://www.20thcenturydirect.com.

Creative Memories has top-notch scrapbook albums sold through a network of home representatives. Contact: (800) 468-9335. On the Internet: http://www.creativememories.com.

Exposures offers an impressive collection of quality albums in many sizes and designs. This company will also personalize the cover and spine of your album. Call for catalog. Contact: (800) 222-4947.

Hallmark stationary stores have albums in a variety of designs.

Pioneer has a good selection of albums and other related materials. Contact: (818) 882-2161. On the Internet: http://www.pioneerphotoalbums.com.

Recipes Shared Organization Kit is a book of pre-designed pages with room for handwritten recipes and memories. Contact: (800) 642-6762.

Planning for Multiple Copies

Do you plan to produce multiple copies of your keepsake, perhaps for members of your family, club, or organization? Here are three alternatives:

Send each person a copy of the completed keepsake materials. They can then buy their own album or binder and insert the keepsake materials themselves.

Ask each person to contribute to the cost of their album. You then buy all the albums, create the cookbooks, and provide the completed masterpieces to everyone.

Use a local copy service. Compare prices of reproduction, binding, and cover alternatives with various local copy services and printers.

Pick Your Pages, Fill Your Pockets

Some albums are unbound, with the pages sold separately. This is a distinct advantage over albums with sewn-in pages because you can choose the type of page you prefer, and add more pages if you need them. You can protect your completed pages from spills, splashes, and fingerprints with acid-free transparent polypropylene or mylar sheets, commonly called "page protectors" or "pocket pages" because they are made with one or more see-through pockets into which you slip your completed keepsake materials.

With full-page pockets, you place two completed cookbook pages back-to-back and slip them into each of the pockets.

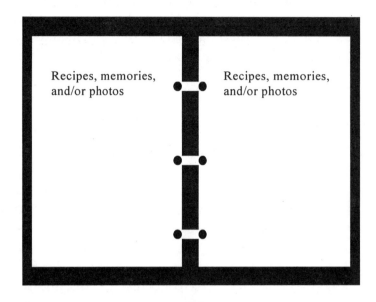

Some page protectors have multiple pockets (center and bottom examples).

To use these pages, just size your keepsake materials to fit into each of the pockets.

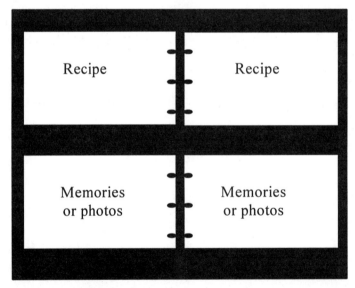

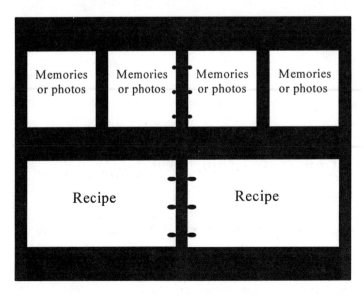

Tips 'n Tools
You can protect your photos even if you don't use page protectors. **Random Mount Protective Photo Holders** by C.R. Gibson are individual mini-pockets you can stick onto your pages. Just slide your photo or drawing inside one of these clear holders, peel off the adhesive backing, and stick it to a page.

Do It Yourself

☐ Decide whether you want to use a one-page or a two-page format.

☐ Determine whether you want to create a simple keepsake of just recipes, or whether you'll include memories and/or visual images as well.

☐ Look at several different types of albums and binders. Choose one that works well with your theme and page format.

☐ If you buy an unbound album, buy page protectors also.

Next step: Collect your recipes.

COLLECTING AND ORGANIZING YOUR MATERIALS

"When someone is born, wed or buried, there food will be, giving sustenance, making one feel secure. Food is the vehicle of love that is passed on in an Italian family, generation after generation. It is tradition."—Mary Ann Esposito, *Ciao Italia*

5. COLLECT RECIPES

In This Chapter:

- Finding Family Recipes
- Collecting Information from the Family
- Setting Clear Expectations
- Using Antique Recipes
- Adapting Recipes
- Other Recipe Sources
- Do It Yourself

Recipes are the heart and soul of your keepsake cookbook. Your family's unique recipes and related traditions are links to a broader heritage. They represent shared sources of sustenance, comfort, joy, and celebration. Whether your family tastes run to hot dogs or grilled pheasant, recording your recipes preserves an important piece of your heritage that can be passed from one generation to the next.

Finding Family Recipes

Start with a bit of detective work. Here are some tips for collecting family recipes and related memorabilia for your keepsake.

1. **Start with the obvious.** Begin by collecting family recipes you have or already know about: Mom or Dad's specialties or the foods you immediately associate with family dinners, Sunday brunches, picnics, holidays, special family celebrations, or childhood

sleepovers with your grandparents. But don't limit your recipes to special occasions. Include the ordinary, everyday foods that are, or have been, your family staples. Crusty macaroni and cheese hot from the oven. Fresh-baked bread slathered with butter. Burgers and hot dogs from the barbeque. Sunday pot roast. Crisp sugar cookies cut into holiday shapes and coated with sweet icing.

2. **Search your memories.** Once you've jotted down or collected all the obvious recipes that come to mind, dig deeper into your memory. When you close your eyes and think about the foods from your childhood, what do you recall? How were foods prepared, who prepared them, or how were they were served? What customs or traditions were observed at the family dinner table, family gatherings, special occasions, and holidays? How about the stories you heard as you were growing up? Mom's account of her hilarious *faux pas* as she struggled to perfect the family's traditional *cacciatore*? The time your dad accidentally added egg nog to the cream of tomato soup. Write down everything you remember.

3. **Ask the family to spill the beans.** When you've written down everything you can remember, encourage relatives to do the same. Ask them to supply everything they know about a family recipe or related tradition. If they have a recipe for Aunt Tilly's apricot preserves, do they have a photo of Aunt Tilly or an old letter she wrote describing the apricot harvest at canning time? Find out as much about the recipes as you can—the ingredients, preparation, and background, and any anecdotes, folklore, or stories that go with them.

You're digging for culinary buried treasure: any information about your family's foods and related traditions is wealth found.

Do they know the origin of a particular dish? How long has it been in the family? How has it been modified over the years to appeal to current tastes or lifestyles? Was something in particular served as an accompanying dish? Have the men in the family always prepared a specific dish? If so, why? Do they remember any recipes that were passed on by word of mouth and never written down? You're digging for culinary buried treasure: any information about your family's foods and related traditions is wealth found. Sort through all these contributions, match them to your own recipes, and decide which to include in your keepsake.

A family reunion is a perfect opportunity to gather recipes, reminisce about family history, and record special memories. You may want to provide a questionnaire in advance and ask relatives to complete it and bring it to the reunion. Or ask family members to bring copies of their recipes to the reunion. Incorporate a "memory session"—what one individual recalls often sparks the memories of others.

No reunion planned? Creating a keepsake cookbook is a great reason to schedule a family get-together!

4. **Become the family snoop.** Search through old letters, diaries, genealogy records, and cookbooks to which you have access. Snoop up in the attic, down in the basement, and look through those old dusty family albums. Along the way, you might uncover some fascinating unknown family history.

Collecting Information from the Family

Providing instructions that are clear and concise will help limit the amount of rework necessary to correct the contributions of others.

There are two ways to collect recipes for your keepsake from family members: you either do most of the work yourself, or you direct the family to collect and develop materials according to your instructions.

Method #1—You do most of the work. Ah, but what wonderful work it is! With this method you are collector, author, editor, graphic designer, and publisher. This method requires more of your time; in the long run it's the most efficient option because it provides a single point of control—you. Ask family members to provide recipes and other information for the keepsake. Compare the materials they give you with everything you've developed or collected on your own. Weed out duplicates, combine different memories about the same recipe, and correct any spelling, grammatical, or other errors.

Method #2—Let others do most of the work. With this method, you provide pre-formatted pages to which relatives add their recipes, memories, photos, or other materials. It's a good idea to avoid duplication of recipes *before* contributors submit their materials. Ask what recipes each person plans to contribute. Resolve any duplicate submissions, then provide pre-formatted album pages to everyone.

You'll have to correct or return any material that needs editing or clarification (you can't read a single word of Cousin Robert's chicken-scratching!), or rewritten (Grace used "T" for tablespoon while everyone else followed your instructions to spell out "tablespoon").

In any case, providing instructions that are clear and concise will help limit the amount of rework necessary to correct contributions. You then put the pages in order, add your cover, title page, table of contents, and section pages, and insert them all into your album.

Tips 'n Tools
If you have a large family, consider sharing the tasks of creating your keepsake cookbook with other family members. Form a family committee and assign tasks to different individuals, or invite everyone over for lunch or dinner to stir up a few memories and enjoy some of those traditional recipes. Consider tape recording the conversation, then later transcribing any useful recipes and memories.

Setting Clear Expectations

Whether you use Method #1 or Method #2, you're more likely to receive the type of information you want if your instructions are clear and concise. Make this exercise as easy as possible for your contributors; you'll save time and frustration—yours and theirs—in the long run. Be clear about the following items:

Share your plans. Give family members an overall sense of what you're trying to accomplish with your keepsake. Share your title, theme, and tone. Describe other materials you have in mind.

Make this exercise as easy as possible for your contributors; you'll save time and frustration— yours and theirs—in the long run.

Specify the format to be used. Do you want typed or handwritten recipes? If they're handwritten, do you care what color ink is used? Is it okay to use either cursive or printing? Provide the acid-free pens you would like contributors to use. Do you want all terms and measurements spelled out? What standard recipe terms or abbreviations you would like everyone to use?

▶   See the Appendix for a list of standard cooking terms and abbreviations you can provide to your contributors.

State the turnaround time. Be clear about when the material should be returned to you. Be sensitive to the demands on family members' time; life is hectic and everyone has a busy schedule. You'll get much better information if you give people sufficient time to be thoughtful about your request.

Method of return. Mention whether you'll pick up the information, if relatives should bring their contributions to a family gathering, or mail them to you (include a self-addressed, stamped envelope with sufficient postage).

If some of your contributors have access to computers, why not provide your request on disk or by e-mail? Ask contributors to return the information to you in the same way. If you're using Method #2, include your pre-formatted pages. At least you'll have some of the information established in your computer. You can easily format materials as you need them, but much of the typing will already be completed. You can use conventional methods to deliver or mail materials to contributors who don't have computers.

Using Antique Recipes

If you're fortunate enough to discover antique or original recipes, by all means incorporate them into your keepsake. Great Aunt Emmaline's recipe for sassafras tea, distant Cousin Albert's Civil War-era recipe for jerky, or Great Uncle Micholov's instructions for *perogi* will make unique additions to your keepsake.

If you're lucky enough to have an antique recipe, display a copy of the original by itself or with a contemporary translation.

Recipe and translation courtesy of Terry Nutter

Tart in Ymbre Day

"Take and perboile oynoun and erbis and presse out the water and hewe her smale. Take grene chese and bray it in a morter, and temper it up with ayren. Do therto butter, safroun and salt, and raisouns corouns, and a litel sugur with powdour douce, and bake it in a trap, and serve it forth."

-Forme of Cury, late 14th century

Tart On Ember Day

This medieval onion-cheese quiche replaced meat on Ember Days (three sets of special days of abstinence occuring four times a year in the Catholic calendar).

Take and parboil onion[s] and herbs, and press out the water, and chop them small. Take green cheese and grind it in a mortar, and temper it up with eggs. Add butter, saffron, and salt, and currants, and a little sugar with powder douce, and bake it in an open crust, and serve it forth.

Notes: Green cheese probably refers to a fresh (as opposed to aged) cheese. A powder douce included sugar and spices—possibly ginger, cinnamon, mace, and cloves.

You can also adapt an antique or original recipe for practical use.

Distant cousin Agnes Stracatto was the wife of a Confederate colonel. With Civil War muskets and cannons booming in the distance, she kept her kitchen staff busy 'round the clock to feed the weary soldiers who used her home as a command base. This is an adaptation of her bean soup. Her version, made by the gallon, included salt pork and homegrown greens.

Agnes Stracatto's Confederate Bean Soup
-Serves 8-

Rinse and soak overnight in enough water to cover:
   1 ½ c. dried beans
Drain the beans and put them into a large pot with:
   8 cups cold water
   Ham hock or other meaty bone
Bring to a boil, then reduce heat and simmer about 1 ½ hours or until the beans are tender.
Remove bone and skim fat from surface of soup.
Remove meat from bone and chop finely. Add back to pot.
Add to pot:
   1 large onion, diced
   2 large potatoes, peeled and diced
   2 stalks celery, chopped
   2 cloves garlic, minced
   Salt and pepper to taste
Simmer until potatoes are tender, about 30 minutes.
Remove from heat and purèe in a blender or food processor.

Tips 'n Tools
Copy antique recipes onto acid-free paper, then include the copy in your cookbook. Carefully store the original.

Adapting Recipes

When collecting materials for your keepsake, you may come across a recipe that, for one reason or another, needs to be adapted or modified. This is often the case with antique recipes, or when traditional family recipes are handed down from one generation to the next by word of mouth and never documented. Then it's time to head to the kitchen for trial-and-error testing to accurately state ingredient quantities and yield. Adapting or revising a recipe might be appropriate whenever you want to do one of the following:

- **Clarify or replace imprecise, outdated, or undesirable ingredients:** Ingredients are vague ("add a healthy dose of salt"); unavailable ("mix with three generous drops of Dr. Bailey's Bayou Sorghum"); or undesirable (Great Granny's stew recipe calls for fresh 'possum tails). Maybe you'd like substitute healthier ingredients ("to reduce fat, substitute equal amounts of applesauce for oil").

- **Contemporize outdated language or terms:** "Pank slowly until the vapors rise and the dregs fall to the bottom of the barrel."

- **Modernize technique:** Adapt an outdated technique ("Churn until smooth and creamy") or modify a contemporary recipe for health reasons ("to reduce fat, bake at 350° for 20 minutes instead of frying").

- **Reduce or increase total yield:** You'd like to reduce Aunt Claire's Christmas cookie recipe to produce less than the three-bushel basket yield. Realize that halving or doubling a recipe's ingredients sometimes adversely affects quality. Always test the recipe yourself to ensure satisfactory results.

Adapting recipes means testing, testing, and more testing in the kitchen. Observe the following to ensure your modified recipe can be repeated successfully:

- Measure ingredients exactly. Record each amount precisely before going on to the next one.

- Record each instruction as you complete it, along with any other helpful information regarding consistency, texture, color, or cooking times. "Boil until thick, about 6-8 minutes," is more helpful than "boil until thick."

- Calibrate your oven to be sure the temperature you record is accurate.

Other Recipe Sources

Thanks to a world full of people who love to cook and eat, there are endless sources of recipes. If you're creating a keepsake for yourself or as a gift, consider these resources.

The Internet is the largest single source of recipes and food-related information available.

- **Your own recipe collections.** Organizing your own recipe collection is a good starter project and a practical way to bring some order to all the loose recipes you've collected over the years. Gather up all those 3x5 cards, the sticky notes in the kitchen drawers, and the little bits of paper poking from between the pages of all your cookbooks. You'll never again have to fumble through the kitchen looking for a favorite recipe. No more squinting at tiny print or reading through the gravy stains.

- **Family.** Unless you're not particularly fond of the way Mom bakes chicken, or you would rather avoid Cousin Sue's high-fat desserts, ask family members for their favorite recipes.

- **Friends.** Mention that you're looking for recipes in a particular category and you'll probably get lots more than you can possibly use.

- **Cookbooks.** Check your local library and bookstores for new and used cookbooks. Estate and garage sales can be treasure troves of cookbooks. You may even find an antique cookbook.

- **The Internet.** This is the most prolific single source of recipes and food-related information available. You'll find thousands of recipes from food lovers and experts all over the world. In addition to websites, visit chat groups where participants swap recipes and offer information and referrals for unique and hard-to-find recipes. Read and observe the terms of use for each site. Here are five great recipe sites, each with thousands of recipes. You can search each site by title, category, ingredient, and nutritional information. To find similar sites, search the Internet for "food," "recipes," and "cooking."

  http://www.cyber-kitchen.com   http://www.mymenus.com
  http://www.digitalchef.com   http://recipes.wenzel.net
  http://www.kitchenlink.com

- **Recipe software.** Recipe collections on disk and CD-ROM can be found in computer stores and on the Internet.

- **TV and radio.** Cooking is a hot topic and a ratings grabber. TV and radio talk shows regularly feature guest cooks who provide recipes. Tune in to the TV Food Network for nonstop recipes (or visit their Internet website at http:// www.foodtv.com).

- **Magazines and newspapers.** In addition to various food magazines (*Bon Appetit, Gourmet, Chile Pepper, Cooking Light, Vegetarian Times,* etc.), many nutrition, fitness, gardening, and women's magazines regularly feature recipes. Most regional and national newspapers regularly print recipes and food-related information.

- **Food and beverage manufacturers.** Check for recipes on product containers, packaging, and the backs of boxes. Manufacturers frequently provide mail-in offers for recipes. Check their websites for recipes and other useful information about their products.

- **Restaurants.** Wish you had a recipe from your favorite restaurant? Just ask for it. Visit the restaurant or write a letter to the manager explaining your purpose and simply request the recipe. Chefs usually don't mind giving out their secrets, as long as the recipes will not be used competitively or for personal gain. Ask for recipes modified for home use, because many restaurants cook in crowd-size quantities.

- **Professional associations.** There seems to be a professional organization or group for every imaginable food and beverage (the American Egg Board, the National Dairy Council, and the Wine Institute, for example). These groups often provide free recipes. Check the Internet or call (800) 555-1212 for a toll-free listing. You can also ask your local librarian for a reference of national organizations.

Tips 'n Tools
Remember to give credit for others' recipes, and to obtain permission before using such recipes for a fundraiser or any cookbook for sale.

Do It Yourself

❏ Collect all the recipes for your keepsake. Request and collect recipes from family members or other contributors. Eliminate any duplicates and make any necessary corrections to recipes submitted by others.

❏ Make copies of any antique recipes you want to use. Carefully store the originals.

❏ Adapt and record any recipes you need to modify.

Next step: Format your recipes.

6. FORMAT RECIPES

In This Chapter:

*   The Four Essential Parts of a Recipe
*   Optional Recipe Information
*   Five Ways to Format Your Recipes
*   Do It Yourself

Well-written recipes always include four basic elements: the title, yield, list of ingredients, and preparation instructions. You may also want to include other information, but always include these four elements.

The Four Essential Parts of a Recipe

Title. Every recipe needs a title that clearly indicates what the recipe produces. Unless your cookbook is intended for family members who understand those "special" names you give to recipes, use titles that clearly describe the end result. "Easy Camping Hash," for example, is far more descriptive than "Fred's Fried Mess," or "Josh's Camping Breakfast."

Yield. State the recipe yield at the beginning or end of all your recipes ("Makes 24 cookies," "Serves 6," or "Yields 4 cups"). It's easier than eyeing the ingredient list and guessing whether you'll have less or more than you need.

Ingredients. List ingredients in the order of use, and accurately state amounts. Note the difference between:

"1 lb. spinach, cooked" and "1 lb. cooked spinach"

The first line refers to spinach that is first measured, then cooked. The second line refers to spinach that is first cooked and then measured. (If you've cooked spinach, you know these are two very different amounts.) List any optional ingredients ("1 cup chopped nuts, optional") and note any differences or additional requirements when using optional ingredients ("using butter instead of margarine produces a smoother, richer sauce").

Instructions. Present your recipe instruction in a clear, logical order. Begin by listing the actions that should be completed prior to the actual preparation: preheat an oven, marinate the chicken, or prepare a sauce or dough prior to the remaining steps. Then list subsequent instructions in the order of completion. Start each sentence with an action verb:

- *Add* two large eggs.
- *Stir* until blended.
- *Heat* until just melted.

Place any information not directly related to the recipe in the recipe introduction, on the facing page, or in a box separated from the recipe text.

Tips 'n Tools
Include the size of the saucepan, baking dish, or mixing bowl needed. Your reader will appreciate instructions to "mix ingredients in a 3-quart saucepan," or "pour batter into a 1-quart baking dish" instead of finding mid-recipe that the container she is using too small.

All recipes should include title, yield, ingredients, and instructions.

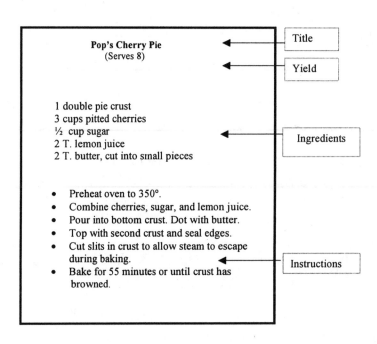

Pop's Cherry Pie ◄——— Title
(Serves 8) ◄——— Yield

1 double pie crust
3 cups pitted cherries
½ cup sugar ◄——— Ingredients
2 T. lemon juice
2 T. butter, cut into small pieces

- Preheat oven to 350°.
- Combine cherries, sugar, and lemon juice.
- Pour into bottom crust. Dot with butter.
- Top with second crust and seal edges.
- Cut slits in crust to allow steam to escape during baking. ◄——— Instructions
- Bake for 55 minutes or until crust has browned.

Optional Recipe Information

In addition to the title, yield, ingredients, and instructions, you can add one or more of the following elements:

Introduction. Called a "headnote" in commercial cookbooks, this sentence or brief paragraph describes the dish ("This chocolate cake forms a rich sauce as it bakes") or shares a bit of the history behind the recipe ("Mom always serves this cake on the ugly blue platter Dad won at the County Fair").

Consider your reader's level of expertise; provide details and directions, and define terms accordingly.

Tips. All cooks appreciate special tips, hints, or information. Use these culinary tidbits to describe any of the following:

- **Serving suggestions.** "Goes well with a tomato-and-cucumber salad," or "Serve with a fruity red wine or chilled Sangria."

- **Preparation options.** "Freeze mixture for up to three months. When ready to use, simmer slowly in covered pan with 1 inch of water for approximately 20 minutes or until tender," or "Bake at 350° for an hour instead of frying."

- **Ingredient substitutions.** "If substituting peanut butter for cream cheese, increase liquids by half," or "For a milder taste, substitute mozzarella for half the Parmesan cheese." Tell the reader how to assess proper consistency, texture, or measure of doneness: "Bake 20 minutes or until top is golden and slightly cracked" is more informative than "Bake for 20 minutes."

- **Unusual terms.** Consider your reader's level of expertise when providing details and directions, and define terms accordingly. Explicitly state, rather than imply, instructions. Writing "Score the top of the loaf by making three very shallow parallel cuts with a sharp, serrated knife" is more instructive than "Score the tope of the loaf." Emphasize any special or important instructions by underlining, italicizing, using bold text, or putting a border around the information.

- **Unusual ingredients.** "One tablespoon chili oil, available in the Oriental section of markets," or "1 cup flaxseed, available at health food stores."

- **Storage information.** "Freezes well for up to six months," or "Refrigerate leftover sauce and veal in separate containers for up to three days."

- **Nutritional analysis.** The amount of calories, fat, cholesterol, or other nutritional elements per serving: "150 calories and 1 gram of fat per serving," or "Contains no cholesterol."

- **Preparation and cooking times.** "Preparation: 15 minutes," "Marinade time: two hours," or "Cooking time: 30 minutes."

Tips 'n Tools

Nutritional analysis is a snap with the right tools. If you're using a recipe software application, check the User's Guide or Help menu to locate this helpful feature. Or you can log onto the Internet and use one of the analysis tools at http://www.mymenus.com, http://www.kitchenlink.com, or http://www.digitalchef.com.

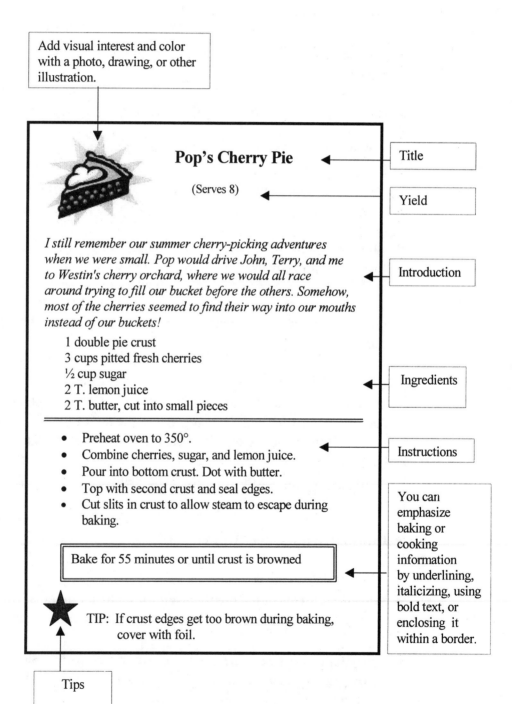

Add visual interest and color with a photo, drawing, or other illustration.

This recipe includes both essential and optional information.

Pop's Cherry Pie

(Serves 8)

I still remember our summer cherry-picking adventures when we were small. Pop would drive John, Terry, and me to Westin's cherry orchard, where we would all race around trying to fill our bucket before the others. Somehow, most of the cherries seemed to find their way into our mouths instead of our buckets!

1 double pie crust
3 cups pitted fresh cherries
½ cup sugar
2 T. lemon juice
2 T. butter, cut into small pieces

- Preheat oven to 350°.
- Combine cherries, sugar, and lemon juice.
- Pour into bottom crust. Dot with butter.
- Top with second crust and seal edges.
- Cut slits in crust to allow steam to escape during baking.

Bake for 55 minutes or until crust is browned

TIP: If crust edges get too brown during baking, cover with foil.

Title

Yield

Introduction

Ingredients

Instructions

You can emphasize baking or cooking information by underlining, italicizing, using bold text, or enclosing it within a border.

Tips

Five Ways to Format Your Recipes

One advantage of creating your own cookbook is the option to choose the style you find most appealing. Look through your favorite cookbooks and notice how essential and optional recipe information is presented. Here are some things to consider:

- How are ingredients and instructions presented?

- Which formats are easiest to read?

- Are recipe ingredients presented in paragraph form, bullets, or numbered steps?

- How are the different essential and optional recipe parts presented?

Consider a style that will appeal and benefit your reader. You might prefer a lot of detail crammed onto your recipe pages, while your sweet little Granny might appreciate an easy-to-read oversized typeface and wide margins. Use a style you find most appealing or create your own. Present information in a reader-friendly format. Whatever format you choose, be consistent; use the same style throughout your cookbook. The following examples show five different recipe formats.

Format 1. Show only essential recipe information.

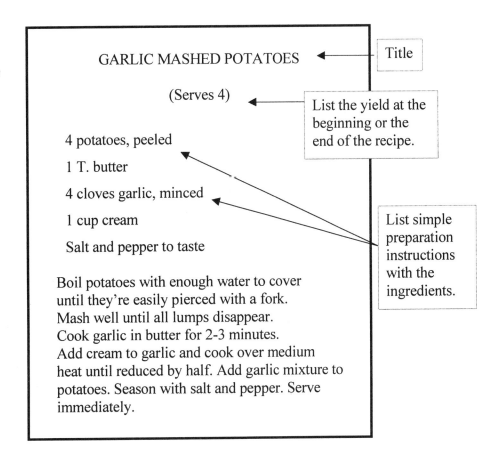

GARLIC MASHED POTATOES ◄——— Title

(Serves 4) ◄—— List the yield at the beginning or the end of the recipe.

4 potatoes, peeled

1 T. butter

4 cloves garlic, minced

1 cup cream

Salt and pepper to taste

List simple preparation instructions with the ingredients.

Boil potatoes with enough water to cover until they're easily pierced with a fork. Mash well until all lumps disappear. Cook garlic in butter for 2-3 minutes. Add cream to garlic and cook over medium heat until reduced by half. Add garlic mixture to potatoes. Season with salt and pepper. Serve immediately.

*Format 2.
Place
ingredients
and instructions
side-by-side,
and position
any optional
information
below.*

GARLIC MASHED POTATOES
(Serves 4)

4 potatoes, peeled

1 T. butter

4 cloves garlic, minced

1 cup cream

Salt and pepper to taste

1. Boil potatoes with enough water to cover until they're easily pierced with a fork.
2. Mash well until all lumps disappear.
3. Cook garlic in butter for 2-3 minutes.
4. Add cream to garlic and cook over medium heat until reduced by half.
5. Add garlic mixture to potatoes.
6. Season with salt and pepper.
7. Serve immediately.

Format the instructions as bulleted or numbered items.

Use a potato ricer for the fluffiest and lightest mashed potatoes. A potato masher, electric beater, or fork will work too. Don't use a food processor: it will make mush of your potatoes.

*Format 3.
List optional
information
alongside the
recipe.*

*M*an has cultivated garlic for more than 5,000 years. The ancient Egyptians and Greeks believed garlic held supernatural powers. Folklore recommends eating garlic to ward off vampires

*L*ike its cousin the onion, garlic is a member of the lily family. Fresh garlic is available all year long. Look for firm heads with tight, papery skins. Store at room temperature away from light.

*G*arlic has been called "the stinking rose." Chew parsley and a few caraway seeds to eliminate the odor.

GARLIC MASHED POTATOES

4 potatoes, peeled
1 T. butter
4 cloves garlic, minced
1 cup cream
Salt and pepper to taste

Boil potatoes in enough water to cover until they're easily pierced with a fork. Mash well until all lumps disappear. Cook garlic in butter for 2-3 minutes. Add cream to garlic and cook over medium heat until reduced by half. Add garlic mixture to potatoes. Season with salt and pepper. Serve immediately.

Serves 4

List instructions in a narrative style.

*Format 4.
Combine the
ingredients in
the instructions.*

GARLIC MASHED POTATOES
(Serves 4)

Boil 4 peeled potatoes with enough water to cover until they're easily pierced with a fork, then mash them until all lumps disappear.

Cook 4 cloves of minced garlic in 1 T. butter for 2-3 minutes.

Add 1 cup cream to garlic.

Cook over medium heat until mixture has been reduced by half.

Add garlic mixture to potatoes.

Season with salt and pepper.

Serve immediately.

*Format 5.
If you have two
or more short
recipes in the
same category,
choose a format
that makes it
easy to show
them on the
same page.*

Bean Dip

1 1-lb. can refried beans
1 c. shredded Cheddar cheese
½ c. chopped green onions
Hot sauce to taste
½ c. chopped cilantro

Combine the beans, cheese, onions, and hot sauce in a saucepan. Stir over medium heat until blended and warmed through. Remove from heat. Stir in cilantro. Serve with corn chips or tortillas.

Makes about 3 cups.

Bleu Cheese Dip

1/3 c. mayonnaise
1 c. sour cream or plain yogurt
1 pkg. (4-oz.) bleu cheese, crumbled
3 T. fresh lemon juice.

Combine ingredients in a blender or food processor. Pulse until smooth. Serve chilled with raw vegetables, crackers, or breadsticks.

Option: Mince 1 clove garlic and add to other ingredients.
Option: Add ½ t. horseradish.

Makes about 2 cups.

Do It Yourself

☐ If you plan to divide your keepsake into different sections, sort your recipes accordingly.

☐ Choose *one* format for all the recipes in your keepsake.

☐ If you *don't want to include* memories, photos, or other graphics in your cookbook, skip to Chapter 9. Read through the entire chapter, then create your recipe pages. (Be sure each recipe in cludes the four basic elements, and any optional information you want to include.)

☐ If you *do want to include* memories, photos, or other graphics in your keepsake, draft your recipes now in the format you like the best. You'll print the final version in Chapter 9.

☐ File the recipes for each category or section into a folder, manila envelope, or page protector. (If you're creating your keepsake entirely by computer, create different folders to store your documents.) To these recipes, you'll add materials as you read through the next two chapters. When you're ready to create your keepsake pages, it will be easy to develop each section one page at a time without sifting through all your materials.

Next step: Record your memories.

"Members of your family will treasure every word you write. To them you are the connection between the remarkable past and the present; in fact, you are history, and history disappears if you don't record it."—Frank B. Thomas

7. RECORD YOUR MEMORIES

In This Chapter:
- Food for Thought: What to Write?
- Finding Your Inspiration
- Getting Your Kids into the Act
- Five Ways To Warm Up
- Tips for Better Writing
- Do It Yourself

Adding personal memories transforms your cookbook from a collection of recipes into a treasured keepsake. Your recipes produce foods that nourish, comfort, and delight. Your stories and anecdotes about your recipes can do the same. Don't worry if you don't think you're a great writer. It's more important to have something on paper, no matter how it's written, than nothing at all. Just do your best. It will probably be much better than you think it is!

Food for Thought: What to Write?

Journaling—the personal memories and other text you write to accompany your recipes—preserves the history and stories behind culinary traditions. Here are a few ways to include journaling in your cookbook.

Record your memories. Write a few lines, a couple of paragraphs, or a full page of stories or anecdotes to capture special memories about a particular food or recipe.

Add photo captions. If you're using photos in your keepsake, always record who is in the photo, where it was taken, and when ("Uncle Stan Wasserstein at the Niagra Falls Café, 1932"). You can expand on these details to include what was occurring during the photo, why it was taken, or how it relates to the recipe.

Use poetry, quotations, song lyrics, and greeting card sentiments. Write your own or record a favorite. Anything that captures your fancy and expresses the sentiment you have in mind is fodder for your pages. Remember that you may use copyright-protected material in your cookbook only if it is for personal use, and not for financial gain. You must obtain permission to use copyrighted materials in a fundraising cookbook, for example.

There are many ways to express yourself or compliment a recipe with writing. Add a quotation, as shown in this two-page format, or fill an entire page with your stories and anecdotes.

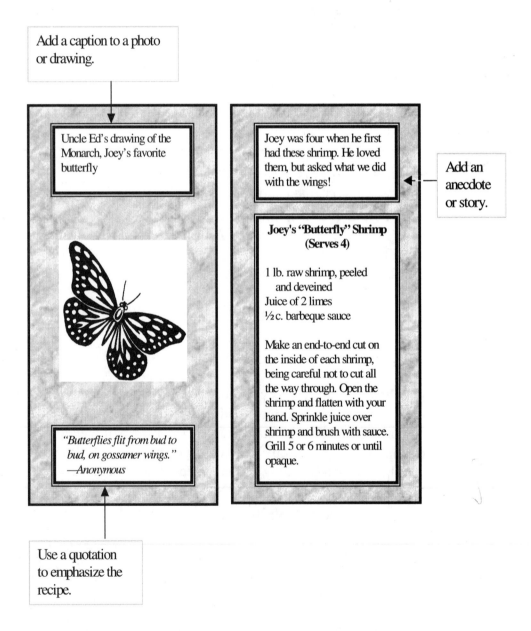

Add a caption to a photo or drawing.

Uncle Ed's drawing of the Monarch, Joey's favorite butterfly

"Butterflies flit from bud to bud, on gossamer wings."
—Anonymous

Joey was four when he first had these shrimp. He loved them, but asked what we did with the wings!

Add an anecdote or story.

Joey's "Butterfly" Shrimp (Serves 4)

1 lb. raw shrimp, peeled and deveined
Juice of 2 limes
½ c. barbeque sauce

Make an end-to-end cut on the inside of each shrimp, being careful not to cut all the way through. Open the shrimp and flatten with your hand. Sprinkle juice over shrimp and brush with sauce. Grill 5 or 6 minutes or until opaque.

Use a quotation to emphasize the recipe.

Finding Your Inspiration

To begin your journaling, think about what you want to convey. How do you want the readers to feel when they read your words? Do you want to create a sense of family pride, paint a literary picture of past times, evoke warm fuzzy feelings, or tickle a funny bone? There are no rules here. Let your imagination, creativity, and heart guide your pen (or your word processor). Just give your creativity free rein and you may be amazed with the results.

For a heritage cookbook, pepper your recipes with memories of your family's foods, related customs, and celebrations. Explain the origin of your family's traditional holiday fruitcake and how the recipe has been passed along to successive generations. Write about traditions you remember from your childhood: the entire family around the dinner table, Dad's Sunday pancakes, or toasting marshmallows under the stars. Describe the sights, sounds, and tastes you recall about particular recipes. The following examples are from two family cookbooks:

Describe the sights, sounds, and tastes you recall about particular recipes.

> *"As a United Nations translator, Dad befriended people from all over the world. On any given evening, our dinner table buzzed with animated conversation—usually in several languages! But everyone understood the simple goodness of Mom's cooking. Her food—baked chicken, pot roast and apple pie—was the universal language that always bridged the cultural and language gaps between us all."*

Life is never all peaches and cream, and chances are your memories aren't either. Don't automatically forego these stories, as long as they fit in with your theme and they don't dwell on the negative. This example from an Italian family's keepsake cookbook accompanies the recipe for their traditional pasta sauce. The recipe preserves a family tradition. The paragraph keeps alive a poignant memory of the family living through a trying time.

> *"I remember Papa shouting 'God be with us' when President Woodrow Wilson declared war against Germany in 1917. Wilson designated Herbert Hoover as Food Administrator. Hoover said we all had to tighten our belts, and encouraged everyone to observe 'wheatless Mondays' and 'meatless Tuesdays.' He urged everyone to eat what he called 'Victory Bread.' We all hated that bread! It was dry and awful. But Mama would make a pot of sauce using whatever ingredients were available. She would simmer onions and tomatoes in water with a little bit of Papa's red wine and add a dash of salt and a pinch of sugar. She called it our 'camouflage soup.' Dunked into Mama's simple sauce, Hoover's Victory Bread wasn't so bad."*

If you're interested in a more contemporary theme, consider the following example. It was excerpted from one couple's travel diary to accompany a recipe from their vacation in France:

"We expected to see meadows of lavender and sample great wines on our trip to Provence, but the highlight of our trip was the food, simply and beautifully presented. This trip changed our blasé attitude towards quiche: every village seemed to have its own unique version. Some used bacon, others included anchovies, but our favorite came from a small nameless café in the village of Murs. We had a fabulous quiche of shrimp, artichokes, basil, and goat cheese. When we asked for the recipe, the proprietress smiled and graciously explained how it was made. Although she spoke little English and we spoke less French, she patiently pointed out the ingredients and cups and spoons of different sizes to indicate appropriate measurements. This recipe, which we adapted at home, is our version of her delicious quiche."

Let the theme you've chosen guide your writing. The following example is one page from a "welcome to the neighborhood" keepsake cookbook. Each neighbor used the same format to record a recipe and information about themselves. (The accompanying recipe is not shown here.) The writing nicely underscores the keepsake theme: it's brief, informative, and welcoming.

WELCOME TO THE NEIGHBORHOOD!

The Miller Family
1539 Kelly Avenue
654-8020

Brian and Julie
Sara (age 8)
Tyler (age 4)

A little about us:
Brian is an engineering manager at Raychem.
Julie volunteers at Central School, where Sara attends, and at Happy Day Preschool, where Tyler terrorizes the sandbox!

We love baseball. Give us a call or come over to enjoy a game anytime (we'll provide the popcorn and peanuts).

Getting Your Kids into the Act

Why not create a keepsake cookbook for your children or enlist them in your project? Let them help make their own first cookbook as they learn to help in the kitchen. Ask them to list or tell you about their favorite foods and why they like each one. What are their least favorites and why? What new foods would they like to try? What are their favorite snacks and how would they prepare them?

While your little ones are still little, keep a pad of paper handy and make a collection of all the unusual and hilarious things they say about food and eating, like the following example:

Add the "grownup" version to your children's recipes. It's also fun to have them add a drawing to the page. They'll have a great keepsake for years to come; one they can pass along to their own children.

Baked Potatoes

Rodney Hernandez
(age 4 - 1987)

To make Baked 'Batadoes get the ones
that look like rocks, then smash 'em
with a fork, then stuff 'em with
'luminin foil, put 'em in the oven, and cook
'em for three days at 600° until they get
dry and bumpy. Put a pound of butter on
the hot part and eat it with your fingers.
You better wear gloves, too."

Mom's version: Wash potatoes and rub skins with butter or olive oil. Prick holes in skin with a fork. Wrap in foil and bake at 350° for one hour, or wrap in plastic wrap and microwave on HIGH for 9 minutes.

As they grow, encourage your kids to add materials to "their" cookbook. (It's also a good way to encourage reading and writing.) Then when they go off to college or move out on their own, you can present them with this wonderful keepsake of their childhood. Hopefully, you will start a new family tradition—one your children will enjoy, maintain, and repeat with your grandchildren.

Five Ways To Warm Up

You don't have to be Shakespeare or Stephen King to journal. All you need is some quiet time, a few memories, and a bit of imagination. Start by focusing on your subject and then let your ideas flow. Write simply and clearly in your own natural style. If you find it difficult to begin, never fear. Try any of the following creative exercises to get you off to a good start.

Go for a practice run. Much like cooking, good writing benefits from practice. The more you write, the easier it gets. One way to practice is to simply pick a topic and write everything that comes to mind about it. Try leading off with one of the following:

- "I remember the time…"

- "I've always wanted to…"

- "If I had a million dollars, I would…"

Or sit in your favorite comfy spot and begin writing about what you see around you: "There's a small puddle of water shining on the white tile counter, and I can see a tiny cobweb perched just under the bottom cabinet near the floor." Observe every little detail. At this point, substance and style aren't important. Just keep writing for a few minutes to rev up your writing engine and get the words on the paper.

Kickstart your memory with photos. Sometimes all you need is a good push to get your writing started. If you have photos of the particular time or activity you want to write about, drag them out. Just looking at them may jog your memory.

▶ Chapter 8 provides information and tips about using photos.

Visualize. Sit down, get comfortable, and close your eyes. Take in a deep breath, then slowly exhale. Now visualize what you want to write about. Put yourself back in the moment, then write down your recollections. Use your senses to recall the place, time of day, and every detail.

One memory often triggers another. If you want to write about your childhood cooking experiences with your grandmother, picture the way she moved around her kitchen, the way she bent over the bowl as she kneaded her pizza dough, and the fragrant, yeasty smell of the pizza as it baked in the oven. That memory may lead you to recall that despite Grandma's warnings, you always burned the roof of your mouth when you just couldn't wait for the pizza to cool. Refine your writing until you're satisfied with the result.

Brainstorm. Pick a subject or topic you want to write about. Using only a few key words, quickly write whatever comes to mind about it. Don't censor as you write. Don't be concerned about using just the right words. Without worrying about spelling, proper tense, or perfect grammar, just start writing everything that comes to mind about those times. The trick is to write without interrupting your flow of thoughts. Let your unedited memories flow freely from your mind to your paper.

Don't censor as you write. The trick is to write without interrupting your flow of thoughts.

Suppose you're having a hard time getting started with memories of cooking with your mother and grandmother. Your brainstorming list might look something like this:

> making *wiener schnitzel* and *latkes*
> feeling loved and secure
> laughing and singing old German songs
> Grandma's stories of her childhood in Munchen
> Mom's faded yellow-and-green plaid apron
> licking the spoon

When you complete your list, go back and take a look at what you've written. Just keep your hand moving; put pen to paper and begin writing whatever comes to mind about the first item on the list. Do the same for the remaining items on your list. As other memories come to mind, write them down too. Then begin editing your work: correct spelling errors, improve grammar, and rewrite and organize what you've written until you're satisfied with the results.

Get it on tape. Use the brainstorming or visualization techniques, but instead of writing your thoughts down, talk into a tape recorder. Speak naturally. Then replay your tape and transcribe what you've said onto paper. If you have a voice-activated word processor for your computer, just start speaking and watch your words appear on the screen in front of you.

Tips for Better Writing

Good journaling paints a vivid mental picture. Here are a few tips to keep in mind as you write.

Start with the easiest memory. Some memories are easier to write about than others. Begin with the ones you remember the most clearly, or the ones that first come to mind. Then tackle the more difficult or unclear memories.

Be specific. Use precise terms to create sharp images. Write "fettuccine" or "cheese ravioli" rather than "pasta." Referring to a triple-layer chocolate cake instead of "dessert" conjures up a more vivid (and accurate) image.

"Punch up" your writing. Use descriptive adjectives; instead of writing "we ate…" try we "gulped," "gobbled," "nibbled," "noshed," or "munched." Choose adjectives carefully to help convey your meaning. Be careful not to overuse descriptive terms.

Use your senses. Describe how things looked, felt, smelled, sounded, or tasted. Write about how the pink, gooey center of the truffle oozed out as you bit through the crisp chocolate coating, or the tickle of silk against your face as you shucked corn.

Develop a definite beginning, middle, and end. When you write your memories or stories, always try to include a beginning, middle, and end. No matter how brief or lengthy they are, always check and edit to make sure your writing has an even flow and includes all the information that is important to the entire story.

Use familiar terms, phrases, or language. If your family always refers to foods, ingredients, or celebrations by special terms, be sure to include them. Use *gnocchi* to describe those little potato dumplings, if that's what your family calls them. Write "Grandmother and her neighbors always bought fresh eggs and cream from The Moo Man, who made his weekly rounds in a rickety old wagon pulled by a big dappled gray horse."

Use dialogue. You can also use dialogue to approximate conversations:

> Mama (aged 9): Why do you have to stir it for so long?
> Nana: Because you have to stir it until it's ready.
> Mama: Well, when is it ready?
> Nana: It's ready when it's ready.
> Mama: But how do you *know* when it's ready?
> Nana: You just know.
> Mama: But *how* do you know?
> Nana: When you've made it 50 times, then you'll know.

Edit. Delete any unnecessary words or phrases that don't add to what you've written. Check for correct punctuation, grammar, and spelling. Here's a good rule of thumb: If you don't need it, get rid of it. It's also a good idea to have someone else (a friend or family member) review what you've written.

Let it rest. Sometimes it's hard to be objective about what you've written. It's a good idea to set your writing aside for a few days, then go back and review it with a fresh outlook. Read it aloud and revise it until you're satisfied.

Tips 'n Tools

To learn more about recording your memories, attend a journaling class at your local college, adult education facility, or crafts store. Visit the library, review Internet sites (search for "scrapbook" and "journaling"), or try one of these helpful tools:

The Memory Triggering Book by Bob Wendlinger (1995 Proust Press). Contact: (888) 534-8989. On the Internet: http://www.triggers.com.

The Art of Writing Scrapbook Stories by Janice T. Dixon, Ph. D. (1998 Mt. Olympus Press). Contact (801) 486-3873. On the Internet: http://www.mt-olympus-press.com.

Turning Memories into Memoirs by Denis Ledoux (1993 Soleil Press). Available from retail and online book stores.

The Journaling Genie by Chatterbox is a nifty tool for handwritten journaling. These stencils help you to write in straight lines, curls, spirals, hearts, and a variety of other shapes. Contact: (208) 286-9517. On the Internet: http://www.chatterboxpub.com.

Do It Yourself

☐   Sort through the memories or journaling provided by family members or other contributors. Make any necessary corrections or changes, and file each one with its corresponding recipe in the folders, envelopes, or page protectors you started in the previous chapter.

☐   Review your remaining keepsake recipes, choosing those you want to write about. Draft and edit corresponding memories or other journaling for each recipe you select. You'll print out the final versions of your memories in Chapter 9. If you find it difficult to get started, use one of the warm-up techniques. When you've completed writing for one recipe, file it with its corresponding memory. Then move on to the next, and the next, until you have written all the memories you want to include in your keepsake.

☐   Collect or draft any quotations, song lyrics, poems, or other writing you want to include in your keepsake. File each with the corresponding recipe.

Do It Yourself (continued)

☐ If you *don't want to include* photos, illustrations, clip art, or other visual images in your keepsake cookbook, skip to Chapter 9. Read through the entire chapter, then create your keepsake pages, using the recipes and journaling from your files.

☐ If you *do want to include* visual images, proceed to Chapter 8.

Next step: Add photos, illustrations, and other images.

"Who would have thought twenty-five years ago that cooking would be a noble career choice and one of America's favorite pastimes?"—Ethan Becker, Foreward, *The Joy of Cooking,* 1997

8. ADD PHOTOS, ILLUSTRATIONS, AND OTHER IMAGES

In This Chapter:

- Using Photos in Your Keepsake Cookbook
- Adding Drawings, Illustrations, and Doodles
- Using Instant Images
- Do It Yourself

A well-known culinary proverb advises that food should please the eye before it pleases the palate. That's also good advice for a keepsake cookbook, because visual images—photographs, illustrations, cartoons, clip art, doodles, or other graphics—break up the monotony of text and add interest, emotion, and color to a cookbook. If you want to test this theory, look at several cookbooks. Your favorites are probably the books with large glossy photos or intriguing illustrations.

Visual images aren't critical to your cookbook, but they can bridge the gap between interesting and exceptional. More importantly, these visuals are a large part of what makes your cookbook a keepsake, because they hold special meaning for the reader.

Begin by considering to what extent you want to include visuals. Do you prefer to spice up your pages with small-scale drawings or full-page photos? Will you include more journaling than visuals or vice versa? Whatever your preference, there are many methods and techniques to add visual effects to your keepsake.

Using Photos in Your Keepsake Cookbook

Because photos are so personal, they are the most effective tools for recalling memories. Your snapshot of that little beach café may mean nothing to most of the people on the planet, but to you and your family, it's a lasting souvenir that instantly transports you back to a special time. Great Aunt Maude's recipe for potato-leek soup will be more meaningful to your family when they see her photo smiling out at them each time they turn to her recipe in the family cookbook.

Use a small photo to introduce a recipe or the recipe contributor.

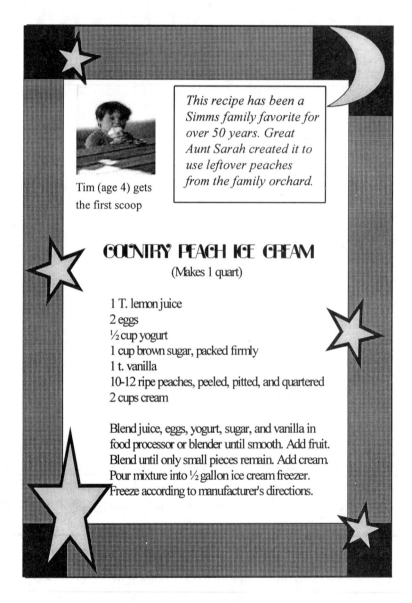

Tim (age 4) gets the first scoop

This recipe has been a Simms family favorite for over 50 years. Great Aunt Sarah created it to use leftover peaches from the family orchard.

COUNTRY PEACH ICE CREAM
(Makes 1 quart)

1 T. lemon juice
2 eggs
½ cup yogurt
1 cup brown sugar, packed firmly
1 t. vanilla
10-12 ripe peaches, peeled, pitted, and quartered
2 cups cream

Blend juice, eggs, yogurt, sugar, and vanilla in food processor or blender until smooth. Add fruit. Blend until only small pieces remain. Add cream. Pour mixture into ½ gallon ice cream freezer. Freeze according to manufacturer's directions.

If you're using a computer to create your keepsake cookbook, there are two very slick methods you can use to incorporate photos onto your pages. If you have digital photos, you can download them directly onto your pages. Alternatively, you can use a scanner to upload photos into your computer.

Then you can reduce or enlarge the photos and position them anywhere on your page. Of course, you can also mount photos directly to your cookbook pages with acid-free double-sided tape, adhesive strips, mounting corners, or glue. If you're using album pages with pockets, you'll cut your photos to fit into the pockets and slip them right in. Here are other techniques you can use with photos:

Cropping. Before mounting your photos, "crop" or trim away any portion that isn't needed or detracts from the main subject. Use this simple technique to improve a less-than-perfect photo.

Cropping Do's	Cropping Don'ts
• *Before* you crop, position a template over your photo to preview how it will look after it's trimmed. • Draw a line around the template on the photo. (Use a ballpoint pen.) • Cut just *inside* the line you've drawn to keep it from showing on the photo after it's been cropped. • Run a sharp-edged craft knife along the edge of a ruler or template to ensure straight photo edges. • Use fancy-edged scissors to give your cropping a special trim.	• Crop heirloom or irreplaceable photos. Use one of the following techniques instead: a. Use a scanned or digital copy of the photo. b. Take a photo of the photo. c. Have a reprint made. Accidents happen; if you make a mistake, you'll have a spare copy. d. Mount the photo to your page, then cut a paper frame and position it over the photo, covering the unwanted portions. Use photo corners to attach the photo to the frame. • Crop Polaroid photos. They're made of 23 paper layers that fall apart when cut. Use one of the methods described above instead.

Silhouetting. Draw attention to a particular photo subject or create a 3-D effect by silhouetting: cut around the perimeter of the subject, then mount it directly onto your page. Silhouetting also works well for combining photo elements. If you want to include a picture of your kids at the beach, for example, but don't have any adequate photos, you can silhouette pictures of your kids, then superimpose the silhouettes over a picture of a beach.

A star silhouette cut from patterned paper.

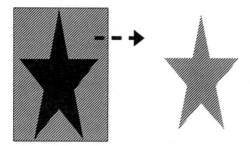

Use the cookie cutter technique. Perk up a page by cutting your photos into different shapes to compliment your overall theme or a particular recipe. Cut photos of your kids into circles or ovals to represent a pile of cookies. Draw in a dish and add a recipe for your favorite cookie recipe. Make a family tree with pictures of family members cut into apple, leaf, or flower shapes. You can actually use cookie cutters or make your own templates: draw or trace the shape onto cardboard or construction paper, then cut it out.

Tips 'n Tools

Does your creativity need a nudge? Look for these tools in scrapbook and photo stores.

Pebbles in My Pocket makes over 20 different styles of decorative photo corners. Contact: (800) 438-8153. On the Internet: http://www.pebblesinmypocket.com.

Want to remove a photo from an old album to use in your keepsake? Check your craft store for **un-du** adhesive remover from Doumar Products. It safely removes adhesives without staining your photo.

Use imaging software to edit, rotate, resize, or crop your photos. Two popular, easy-to-use products are **PhotoDeluxe** by Adobe Systems, Inc. Contact: (800) 888- 6293, and **Picture It!** by Microsoft. Contact: (800) 426-9400.

Adding Drawings, Illustrations, and Doodles

If you have a knack with a pen or pencil, try your hand at small-scale, simple illustrations: draw one of the recipe's main ingredients or twine a flowering vine up the side of your page. Doodle a few colorful fishies swimming around your recipe for grilled halibut. On a larger scale, try full-page caricatures of family members, a scene from a favorite vacation, or include your child's artistic masterpiece. A variety of stencils are available to help you quickly add in perfectly drawn figures, shapes, and designs. If you intend to add your own illustrations, but don't want to create a drawing for every page, you can design a master page, then duplicate it for other pages, or limit your artwork to the introductory section pages of your cookbook. Here are a few tips for adding illustrations:

- Create your drawings on a separate piece of paper and make any changes before drawing directly onto your keepsake page.

- Use acid-free pens and pencils. Avoid using chalk, charcoal, pens, or other pencils that may smear when the book is closed.

- Trace figures from coloring books, magazines, or other sources.

- Use a copier to reduce or enlarge images.

Add visual interest to your page with an illustration of one of the recipe ingredients.

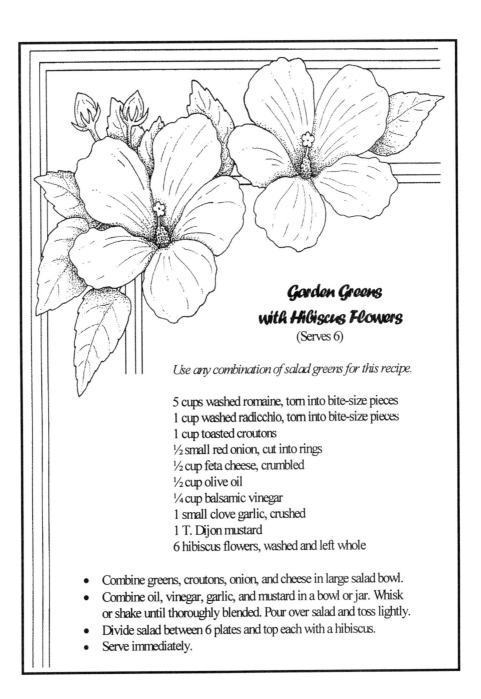

Garden Greens
with Hibiscus Flowers
(Serves 6)

Use any combination of salad greens for this recipe.

5 cups washed romaine, torn into bite-size pieces
1 cup washed radicchio, torn into bite-size pieces
1 cup toasted croutons
½ small red onion, cut into rings
½ cup feta cheese, crumbled
½ cup olive oil
¼ cup balsamic vinegar
1 small clove garlic, crushed
1 T. Dijon mustard
6 hibiscus flowers, washed and left whole

- Combine greens, croutons, onion, and cheese in large salad bowl.
- Combine oil, vinegar, garlic, and mustard in a bowl or jar. Whisk or shake until thoroughly blended. Pour over salad and toss lightly.
- Divide salad between 6 plates and top each with a hibiscus.
- Serve immediately.

Create or choose a drawing that emphasizes your recipe and journaling.

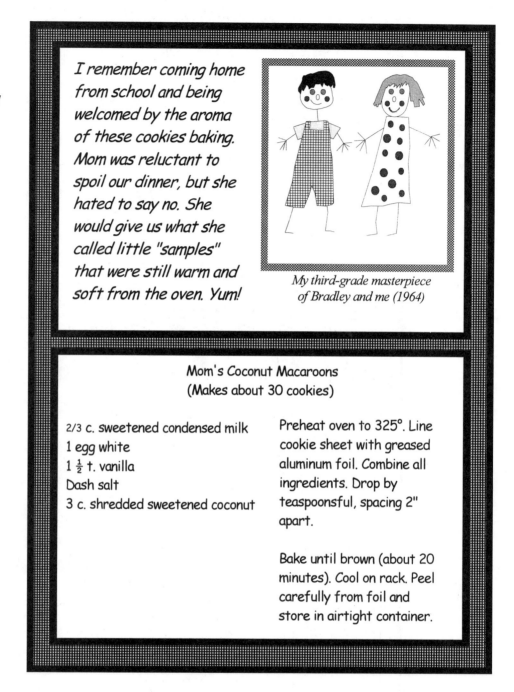

I remember coming home from school and being welcomed by the aroma of these cookies baking. Mom was reluctant to spoil our dinner, but she hated to say no. She would give us what she called little "samples" that were still warm and soft from the oven. Yum!

My third-grade masterpiece of Bradley and me (1964)

Mom's Coconut Macaroons
(Makes about 30 cookies)

2/3 c. sweetened condensed milk
1 egg white
1 ½ t. vanilla
Dash salt
3 c. shredded sweetened coconut

Preheat oven to 325°. Line cookie sheet with greased aluminum foil. Combine all ingredients. Drop by teaspoonsful, spacing 2" apart.

Bake until brown (about 20 minutes). Cool on rack. Peel carefully from foil and store in airtight container.

Using Instant Images

In addition to (or instead of) photos and illustrations, you can use "off-the-shelf" visual images to add interest and color to your keepsake pages.

Clip art. Create simple or intricate designs, frames, borders, and cartoons with computer clip art. Insert these images directly onto your pages, then enlarge or reduce the images to the size you want and position them anywhere on your page.

Using clip art and a word processing application, you can easily apply the same border to all your cookbook pages. Refer to your application's User's Guide or Help menu for details. Here are a few common sources for clip art collections:

- Computer stores.

- On the Internet (search for "clip art").

- Craft and scrapbooking stores and catalogs.

Clip art is a quick and inexpensive way to add colorful images to your pages. (The bold print on this section page indicates recipes that are included in the section.)

*Our 1977 Maui vacation was a fabulous blend of spectacular sunsets, beautiful beaches, and wonderful new foods. We fell in love with fresh grilled **opi** and **mahi mahi,** served with just a hint of lime and ginger.*

*The fish was always fresh. It was usually served with a **fruit relish** made of local produce. Each restaurant seemed to have its own version. Of the many relishes we sampled, our favorite was made with papaya, avocado, orange, and red onion. The colors and tastes were spectacular!*

*We also discovered Maui onions. We were amazed by their sweet, mild taste. Since our island vacation, one of our new favorite salads is sliced fresh **tomatoes** and **Maui onions** in a simple **vinaigrette dressing,** served with a crisp-crusted **cheese bread** hot and fragrant from the oven.*

Stencils, stamps, stickers, and die-cuts. Create instant artwork, borders, frames, and accents with these quick, easy-to-use visual images. Use them to make quick and colorful borders or frames, or to accent a recipe or memory. Die-cuts are medium-weight papers that are pre-cut into every conceivable shape and size. Look in stores and catalogs that sell stationary, craft, or scrapbooking supplies.

Sea horse stickers and clip art are combined on this page to create a tropical background for the recipe.

MAUI RELISH
(Makes about 2 1/2 cups)

1 fresh pineapple, diced
1 c. avocado peeled, seeded, and diced
1/4 c. red bell pepper, seeded and diced
1/2 c. red onion, diced
1/4 c. fresh cilantro, chopped
Juice of 1 lime

Combine the pineapple, avocado, pepper, and onion in a medium-sized serving bowl. Toss gently with cilantro and juice! Serve at room temperature or store covered in refrigerator for 1-2 days.

Do It Yourself

☐ Sort and select the photos you want to include in your keepsake. Draft and edit a caption for each photo that doesn't have a written memory. File the photos and captions with the corresponding recipes. You'll crop your photos in Chapter 9.

☐ If you postponed writing any memories until you selected your photos, draft and edit those memories now, and file them with the corresponding recipes.

☐ Collect or draft illustrations. File each one with the corresponding recipe. In Chapter 9, you'll copy final drawings or tracings directly onto your cookbook pages.

☐ Gather stickers, clip art, or any other images you plan to include.

Your folders, envelopes, or page protectors should now include recipes, memories, and visual materials, all organized according to the sections in your cookbook.

Next step: Create your pages.

PUTTING IT ALL TOGETHER

"A cheerful heart hath a continual feast."—Proverbs 15:15

9. CREATE YOUR PAGES

In This Chapter:

- Select Background Papers
- Add Page Borders (Optional)
- Position Materials on Page
- Compile a Temporary Index (Optional)
- Create the Remaining Recipe and Memory Pages
- Do It Yourself

At this point you have all your keepsake materials together in files corresponding to the sections of your cookbook. Within each section file, your written memories, photos, and other materials should be matched up with a recipe. Now you're ready to combine all these elements to create the pages of your keepsake. Read through this entire chapter, then follow the steps in the Do It Yourself section.

Note: If you still haven't purchased an album or binder, do so now. You'll avoid creating cookbook pages which then might not fit into the album or binder you choose.

Select Background Papers

Thanks to an increasing interest in scrapbooking, buying these page-size papers is like shopping for fabric: you'll find every conceivable color, shade, theme, and pattern. Use a whole page as background for recipes, journaling, or artwork, or cut a sheet of paper into borders and frames as described later in this chapter. Computer stationary also works well.

Tips 'n Tools

Use your computer to make your own background paper. Just import and repeat a photo or clip art image over and over across the page. Or try **Behind It All** by Homespun Software, a software application specific-ally designed to customize background sheets. Contact: (800) 727-2427. On the Internet: http://DSAmerica.com/homespun.

SticSure makes papers with adhesive backing. Use the entire sheet, or cut it into border strips, frames, or other shapes. Then just strip off the backing and stick each shape to your background page. Contact: (714) 572-1213.

Add Page Borders (Optional)

Borders add color and interest to your cookbook and help to define the interior page space. Add borders *before* you position any other materials onto the page. Use fancy-edged scissors or templates to make wiggly, squiggly, or wavy borders. Try using your word processor or clip art applica-tion to easily repeat and duplicate borders on each page. You can also purchase adhesive borders in various designs; just remove the backing and stick them to your page. Or use one of the following techniques to make borders from decorative papers. (You can use the same techniques to make frames for your recipes, memories, and photos)

To make a border from pre-designed paper, center and mount your recipe, memo-ries, or photo onto the paper. The portion of the paper left uncovered forms a page border.

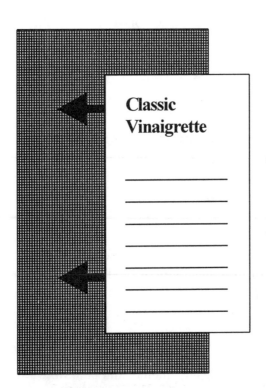

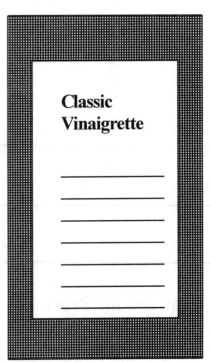

Use embroidery scissors or a craft knife to carefully cut away the center portion of a sheet of background paper or stationary. Use photo tape to mount the remaining border to a background page.

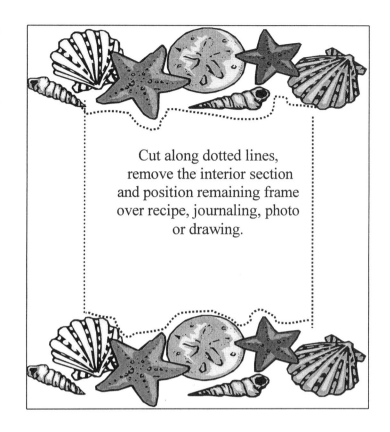

Cut along dotted lines, remove the interior section and position remaining frame over recipe, journaling, photo or drawing.

Use a clip art border to compliment a recipe.

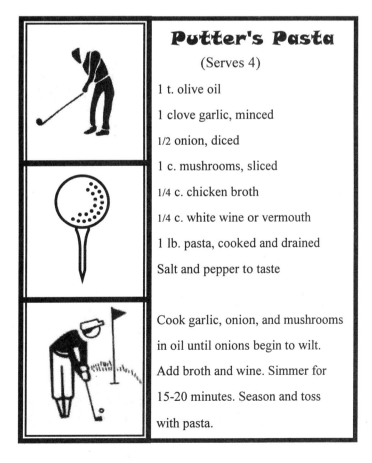

Putter's Pasta

(Serves 4)

1 t. olive oil

1 clove garlic, minced

1/2 onion, diced

1 c. mushrooms, sliced

1/4 c. chicken broth

1/4 c. white wine or vermouth

1 lb. pasta, cooked and drained

Salt and pepper to taste

Cook garlic, onion, and mushrooms in oil until onions begin to wilt. Add broth and wine. Simmer for 15-20 minutes. Season and toss with pasta.

Tips 'n Tools

Borders & Beyond Idea Book by Toni Nelson and Beth Reames contains 52 pages of ideas for page borders. Available in craft and scrapbooking stores. On the Internet: http://www.scrapramento.com.

Position Materials on Page

Move materials around on the page until you have the placement you want. Leave generous margins around all page edges and avoid crowding too much onto one page. When you're satisfied with the placement, print or mount the materials to the background paper. If you want to include any drawings or tracings, do them now.

Compile a Temporary Index (Optional)

If you plan to create an index, first make a temporary listing. As you complete each page, give it a preliminary number. Then list any index items on your temporary index, noting the preliminary page number. Do the same with each page you complete. When all your pages are finished and in order, you can then renumber your pages (if necessary) and finalize your index.

▶   You'll assign final page numbers and finalize your index in
      Chapter 10.

Create the Remaining Recipe and Memory Pages

Repeat the same process to create each of your remaining recipe and memory pages. Working with your sorted materials, complete each page within a section, then move on to the next section, until you've completed all your recipe and memory pages.

▶   You'll create your cover and any optional pages in Chapter 10.

Tips 'n Tools

You'll find a plentiful supply of books, software, and other tools with ideas and designs for page layouts. Here are two examples:

Creative Photo Albums Deluxe by DogByte Development contains 490 page layouts and can crop photos into more than 30 shapes. Contact: (800) 936-4298. On the Internet: http:/www.dogbyte.com.

The Print Shop by Broderbund is a popular software application that contains almost 5,000 pre-designed layouts. Contact: (800) 548-1798. On the Internet: http://www.printshop.com

Do It Yourself (for journals and albums with sewn-in pages)

If you're using a journal or other type of bound album, you won't be able to rearrange the order of your completed pages. So, before actually writing directly onto your pages, it's a good idea to calculate the total number of pages you'll need, and the order in which they will appear. This extra effort is well worth the time.

❑ Be sure your keepsake materials for each page are grouped together. If you want to include an index, draft a list of items from your grouped materials now.

❑ Draft your cover page.

❑ Draft your dedication page, section pages, and appendix if you plan to include any of them.

❑ Draft your table of contents. Don't list any page numbers yet.

❑ Put all the materials listed above in the order you want them to appear in your cookbook. Considering the size of your album pages, estimate the total pages you'll need. (Be sure to include index pages in your estimate, if appropriate.) If you want all of your recipe sections to appear on right-hand pages, as they commonly do in commercial cookbooks, take this into consideration when estimating your page count.

❑ Working with your filed keepsake materials for one page at a time, transcribe your draft materials onto your journal or album pages. Complete each page in order from the front to the back of the journal or album. If you want to add borders to your pages, draw or stick them to your pages *before* adding other materials.

❑ Assign a number to each page, beginning with the first section page or recipe page. (Don't number the cover page or table of contents.)

❑ Record the appropriate page numbers in your table of contents and index.

Congratulations! You've completed your keepsake cookbook. (You don't need to complete the steps in Chapter 10.) Now it's time to start planning your next culinary masterpiece. Reread the previous chapters or use the handy step-by-step checklist in the appendix.

Do It Yourself (for albums and binders with loose pages)

Create your cookbook pages one at a time, working with the materials you've collected. Create each page within a section, then move on to create the pages within each of the remaining sections.

Follow these steps to complete each recipe and memory page:

☐   Select your background paper.

☐   Add a border to the page (optional).

☐   Position and write, type, draw, trace, mount, or print your materials to the background paper. If you're using page pockets, resize each component as necessary to fit into the pockets.

☐   Add a preliminary page number to each recipe and memory page as it is completed. List the recipe titles and other items on your temporary index (optional).

Next step: Add finishing touches and assemble your cookbook.

10. ADD FINISHING TOUCHES AND ASSEMBLE YOUR COOKBOOK

In This Chapter:

- Put Your Pages in Order
- Create the Section Pages (Optional)
- Develop the Appendix (Optional)
- Number Each Page (Optional)
- Create the Table of Contents
- Produce the Index (Optional)
- Create Your Title Page and/or Dedication Page (Optional)
- Develop the Cover Page
- Protect Your Pages
- Place All Completed Pages into Your Album

You now have a stack of completed recipe and memory pages waiting to be assembled. In this chapter you'll create the remaining parts of your cookbook and put everything together. You're just a few steps away from a completed keepsake cookbook.

Do It Yourself

☐ **Put your pages in order.** Put all your completed recipe and memory pages in order. If you plan to divide your cookbook into sections, arrange the pages in the first section, then do the same with subsequent sections until you're satisfied with the order of all your pages.

Do It Yourself (continued)

☐ **Create the section pages (optional).** Develop a section or divider page for each section in your cookbook. Insert each section page *in front of* the corresponding section of recipes.

☐ **Develop the appendix (optional).** If you want to include any other information that doesn't directly relate to a specific recipe (menus, shopping plans, cooking terms, or measurement charts, for example), create an appendix. Place the appendix *behind* your other completed pages.

☐ **Number each page (optional).** If you plan to include page numbers on your table of contents or you want to create an index, assign a number to each page. When you're satisfied with the order of your pages, number each page, including the section pages before each category of recipes. Use small adhesive numbers or an acid-free pen to position the numbers.

☐ **Create the table of contents.** Be sure all entries actually appear on the page indicated before printing or writing your final version. Place the table of contents *in front* of all your other completed pages. Don't number your table of contents.

☐ **Produce the index (optional).** Working with the temporary index you created in the previous step, check to be sure all entries actually appear on the pages indicated. Make any necessary corrections. If you want to list any of your appendix topics in your index, do so now. Place the completed index *behind* all your other keepsake pages. Numbering these pages is optional.

☐ **Create your title page and/or dedication page (optional).** If you want to include either or both of these pages, create them now. Place them *in front* of your table of contents. Don't number these pages.

☐ **Develop the cover page.** Include your title and any other text, photos, or images. Slip your completed cover page into the front pocket of your album or place it *in front* of your completed pages.

☐ **Protect your pages.** Insert each completed page into a full-sized page protector. If you created your cookbook pages using page pockets, insert your cover, title page, dedication page, table of contents, section pages, appendix, and index pages into full-size page protectors.

Do It Yourself (continued)

☐ **Place all completed pages into your album.** Be careful to maintain the order you've established.

Congratulations! You've completed your first keepsake cookbook. Now it's time to start planning your next culinary masterpiece. Reread the previous chapters, or use the handy step-by-step checklist in the appendix.

MORE IDEAS

"Offerings of food have been breaking down barriers for centuries." — Estee Lauder

11. COOKBOOKS AS PROFITABLE FUNDRAISERS

In This Chapter:

- Rally the Troops
- What to Expect from a Cookbook Publisher
- Why Not Publish It Yourself?
- Plump Up Your Profits
- Build On Your Success

Fundraising cookbooks (often referred to as "community cookbooks") fit the definition of keepsakes: they are mementos of the special people who make up a particular charity, club, community service, team, school, church, or other organization. Keepsakes may also be created to commemorate a special occasion, a unique gathering, an historic anniversary, or a memorable event. Cookbooks make effective fundraisers because they have a built-in core of buyers. Members typically buy copies for themselves (everyone likes to support their organization and to see their own name in print) and enthusiastically urge others to do the same.

Rally the Troops

A fundraiser is best accomplished as a team effort. Start by forming a small committee of dependable volunteers who are willing to stick with the project from beginning to end. You may also want to establish subcommittees to coordinate the planning, production, and marketing of your cookbooks. Here are a few issues to consider before you launch your fundraising efforts:

What is the purpose or overall goal of your fundraising effort? Do you want to raise funds to buy new equipment, fund a trip, make a charitable donation to another organization, or keep your group afloat for another year? Choose a cookbook theme that emphasizes your goal.

How much money do you hope to raise? This information is helpful when calculating how much you can spend to publish your book, how many books you need to sell to reach your goal, and how much to charge for your cookbooks. Set a price that is low enough to encourage people to buy your book, yet high enough to reach your targeted profit. You're more likely to realize greater profits if you strive for a defined goal.

What aspect of your organization would you like to highlight in your cookbook? Do you want to call attention to your philanthropic efforts, your long tradition of service, or the individual and collective growth of your members? Use this opportunity to share the story of your organization with others.

You're more likely to realize greater profits if you strive for a defined goal.

What information would you like members to contribute? How many recipes of what type should each member provide? Do you want them to also include photos, historical information, or stories? If you want them to include memories, do you prefer a sentence with each recipe, or a paragraph, or an entire page?

▶   Use the collection techniques described in Chapter 5.

Include contributions from those who benefit most by your group. If your Little League is trying to raise funds, include letters from the kids describing what the sport means to them. If you're raising money to buy guide dogs for the blind, include testimonials from those who have previously benefited from the dogs.

Will you use a cookbook publisher or publish yourself? Many commercial publishers specialize in fundraising cookbooks. Whether you contract with one of these publishers or put your cookbook together yourself depends on the resources available to you, including volunteers, desktop publishing equipment, and expertise. If your group would rather not undertake the effort required, contact a commercial publisher.

What to Expect from a Cookbook Publisher

Although printing styles, designs, and costs may vary between publishers, most use a standard recipe format for fundraising cookbooks. Generally, you choose the cover and section pages from a variety of the publisher's designs, and add a title page of your own text. The standard recipe format used by most cookbook publishers leaves little or no room for personal text (your memories) or artwork (your photos or drawings).

If you consider using a cookbook publisher, make contact early in your project. You want a publisher who will work with you every step of the way. Call several publishers and request copies of their information kits. Compare costs, page designs, and samples of their work. Request information about different options for containing your publishing costs. Ask for references of other organizations who have produced cookbooks with the publisher, then contact the references to determine how they rate the experience.

Many publishers include lots of extras in the basic publishing price: forms for requesting recipes from contributors, sales tips, planning your project timeline, tips for organizing your recipes, and so on. If you have special requests or other questions, call each publisher to see how they would handle your project. Search the Internet for publishers who specialize in fundraising cookbooks or use the list at the end of this chapter.

Cookbook publishers typically show two or three recipes on each page (below), and limit other text and artwork to the cover and section pages.

Savory Baby Bok Choy   *Helen Jones*

4 baby bok choy
¼ cup soy sauce
¼ cup balsamic vinegar
2 T. chicken broth

Steam bok choy until tender. Combine remaining ingredients thoroughly in small saucepan and heat until warmed through. Pour sauce over bok choy.

Artichokes with   *Glen Watson*
Garlic Mayonnaise

4 artichokes, steamed
1 cup mayonnaise
2 cloves garlic, minced
2 T. Worchestershire
½ t. lemon juice

Combine mayonnaise, garlic, Worchestershire, and lemon juice. Dip artichoke leaves into sauce.

Microwave Onions   *Mae Ready*

4 red or yellow onions
¼ cup chicken broth
2 tablespoons honey
Salt and pepper to taste

Place onions in glass pie plate. Pour in broth. Drizzle honey over tops of onions and sprinkle with salt and pepper. Microwave on HIGH for 8 minutes or until tender when pierced.

Baked Cheese Potatoes   *Jo Moran*

4 baked potatoes
½ cup favorite cheese, shredded
1 t. Dijon mustard
1 green onion, sliced

Scoop potato from skin. Mix potato with cheese and mustard and spoon back into shell. Broil until cheese melts. Top with onions and serve.

Why Not Publish It Yourself?

Your organization or club may already have all the tools needed to create your own keepsake fundraiser: a computer, a printer, and enthusiastic volunteers. Consider using the techniques described throughout this book to publish your own cookbook. Recruit volunteers to donate time, equipment, or expertise in printing or desktop publishing.

You can streamline your efforts by standardizing your page layouts. Limit your pages to two or three simple designs, or create a master page design with a small space for individual drawings, anecdotes, or memories. To save time and effort, strive for a simple design and format.

The most important action you can take is to recruit enthusiastic supporters. A few volunteers with a passion for what you're doing can motivate others and achieve incredible results. Recruit people with computer skills to translate handwritten contributions into computerized text. Look for people who are willing to donate the use of their equipment. Perhaps a member or supporter is willing to donate the use of his copier machine if you buy the paper. Or take your master documents to a discount copy center and have them reproduced and spiral bound. (While spiral binding isn't the best idea for a personal keepsake cookbook, it's a common inexpensive method of binding fundraisers.)

If you have plenty of volunteers, access to a high-speed copier, and a spiral binding tool, consider organizing an assembly line to do the work at no cost. At the most, your costs will be limited to materials. If you can get those donated too, even better.

Include the "who," "what," "why," and "where" of your cookbook on your title page (left). You may also want to add a dedication page to acknowledge contributors and supporters (right).

The
Salsbury Ballet Club

Proudly presents our collection of high-energy, nutritious recipes.

Proceeds from this cookbook will help fund next year's costumes and music.

We gratefully thank you for your continued support.

April 1999

WE'D LIKE TO THANK OUR STARS!

We would like to gratefully acknowledge the time and efforts of the six special people whose commitment, enthusiasm and hard work made this cookbook a reality.

We thank each of you for your unfailing support on behalf of our organization.

John Bohanner   Leslie Stuhr
Jan Omega   Laura Tong
Ben Radison   Kevin O'Shea

With desktop publishing, you can easily and economically create your own fundraiser. Create a master page design and ask contributors to add their recipes and/or comments.

This was a great season! I had fun. I learned a lot, and I made new friends. Whether we won or lost, I knew one of these chili dogs was waiting for me!

Chip Gordon **(shortstop)**

1995 Orion Little League Ballpark Chili Dogs (Serves 6)

6 plump hot dogs
6 hot dog buns
3 c. favorite chili
Chopped onions
Shredded cheddar
  cheese

Simmer hot dogs until warmed through. Grill buns. Split hot dogs and place in buns. Heat chili. Pour over hot dogs, and top with onions and cheese.

Plump Up Your Profits

Fundraising profit is defined by a basic business formula:

SALES REVENUE - COST = PROFIT

You can maximize your fundraising profit in two ways: by increasing sales or reducing costs. The more you can do to accomplish both, the more money you'll raise for your worthy cause.

Increasing Sales

- **Start selling before you publish.** The more you sell, the bigger your profit, so get a headstart before your cookbook is published. Spread the word and create enthusiasm and anticipation as you take advance orders. Provide gift certificates for anyone who wants to purchase your cookbook as a gift for someone special.

- **Increase the number of people who contribute recipes to your fundraiser.** Since contributors buy cookbooks and sell many others by word of mouth, more contributors usually means more sales.

- **Build a sales network.** Ask every member of your organization to buy at least one cookbook (more is better). Urge them to encourage their friends, neighbors, and families to buy cookbooks too (the fundraisers make great gifts). Conduct a contest to motivate members to increase sales. Award donated prizes to the members who sell the most cookbooks. Or show your appreciation and encourage increased sales by providing certificates of appreciation or blue ribbons to every member who sells at least three or four cookbooks (or whatever number your group determines).

- **Promote shamelessly.** Promote your cookbook as much as possible without incurring further cost. Distribute flyers and posters around town, ask other organizations for their support, and mention your cookbook in your group's newsletter. If you're promoting a nonprofit organization, ask whether your local newspaper offers a no-cost ad. Send a news release to newspapers and TV and radio stations. Ask civic leaders and local merchants for their support. Ask every company that does business with your organization or club to buy a cookbook.

If the cause is appropriate, allow your children help with fundraising efforts, especially if the profits will benefit their own activities.

- **Broaden your cause.** Consider combining your fundraising efforts with another organization, then splitting the profits. Or stimulate sales by donating a portion of your proceeds to another cause.

- **Time the sale of your cookbooks to a special event or occasion.** Does your organization conduct or participate in a seasonal or annual bazaar, festival, or other event? Do you have an auspicious anniversary coming up? Plan to have your cookbooks ready in time to take advantage of your captive audience.

- **Get your kids involved.** If the cause is appropriate, allow your children to help with fundraising efforts, especially if the profits will benefit their own activities. Kids are enthusiastic and creative, and they can learn valuable lessons from the experience.

Reducing Costs

This is the other way to improve your profits. If you can increase sales *and* reduce the cost of producing your cookbook, you'll realize even larger gains.

- **Reduce publishing costs.** Publishing is typically the largest cost associated with fundraising. You realize a profit only after you've sold enough cookbooks to offset the cost of publishing. Here are a few ways to minimize that cost:

  a. **Do it yourself.** Use the self-publishing techniques described earlier in this chapter and throughout this book.

b. **Shop around for a cost-effective cookbook publisher.** If you decide to use a cookbook publisher, compare services and shop around for the best rates. Don't be afraid to ask the publishers how they will help you contain your costs.

c. **Solicit donations of materials.** If you decide to self-publish, you can save even more if you're able to secure donations of materials (paper, bindings, etc.). In an ideal situation, volunteers create your fundraiser with donated materials, totally eliminating all production costs. That means every penny of your sales is pure profit.

d. **Don't spend money on advertising.** Create a marketing committee to strategize and publicize. Utilize your member network, flyers, brochures, and other no-cost techniques to spread the word. Ask newspapers and local merchants for their support.

Tips 'n Tools
Remember: You must obtain permission to legally use any copyright-protected material in a cookbook that is sold for profit.

Build on Your Success

When something works well, it bears repeating. Capitalize on your fundraising success with a fundraising sequel. Here are a few tips to guide your subsequent efforts.

Learn from your mistakes. Repeat what worked well on your initial effort, and either fix or eliminate what didn't.

Re-enlist your champions. If you have committee members who were especially motivating last time around, are good at networking, and happen to be all-around go-getters, try your best to recruit them again.

Publish new recipes. Motivate supporters to buy your sequel by including new recipes and other materials. One way to do this is to include a survey at the back of your original cookbook asking buyers what other types of cookbooks they would purchase.

Promote the sequel(s). Make sure that you promote your subsequent effort as a different cookbook, so potential buyers don't think they already have what you're selling. Consider updating your cookbook every two or three years, or developing a series of cookbooks—you can then encourage buyers to buy the entire collection.

Broaden your sales network. Look for ways to increase your sales with each new cookbook. Recontact everyone who bought your original cookbook. Build a mailing list from every sale. Encourage supporters to recommend your book to someone else. Or better yet, ask them to buy a copy for themselves and another for someone else.

Tips 'n Tools

Check your local library for more information on fundraising. To find a publisher who specializes in fundraising cookbooks, search the telephone directory or the Internet for "cookbook publishers" or "fundraisers." Here are five such publishers:

Cookbooks by Morris Press. Contact: (800) 445-6621. On the Internet: http://morriscookbooks.com.

Cookbook Publishers, Inc. Contact: (800) 227-7282. On the Internet: http://www.cookbookpublishers.com.

G&R Publishing Company. Contact: (800) 383-1679. On the Internet: http://www.cookbookprinting.com.

Gateway Publishing Co. Contact: (800) 665-4878. On the Internet: http://www.gatebook.com.

General Publishing & Binding, Inc. Contact: (888) 397-0892. On the Internet: http://www.fundraising-cookbooks.com

"You can't expect a person to dance before he's eaten."—Shalom Aleichem, *Tevye Wins a Fortune*

12. 101 THEMES FOR KEEPSAKE COOKBOOKS

Are you stumped for a cookbook theme? Overwhelmed by the possibilities? This list of 101 possible themes and occasions for keepsake cookbooks may help. You can also choose one of these ideas as a starting point and make it more specific. From the "chili" theme, for example, you might create a cookbook of vegetarian chili recipes.

1. Anniversary
2. Aphrodisiacs
3. Autumn
4. Baby
5. Barbecue
6. Beer
7. Beginning cook
8. Beverages
9. Birthday
10. Blender
11. Bread / Bread machine
12. Breakfast
13. Brunch
14. Camping
15. Candy
16. Canning and preserving
17. Cereal
18. Cheese
19. Cheesecake
20. Chile peppers
21. Chili
22. A child's first cookbook
23. Chocolate
24. Christmas
25. Coffee
26. College student
27. Comfort foods
28. Diner foods
29. Dinner
30. Desserts
31. Dips
32. Easy and quick
33. Edible flowers
34. Eggs
35. Ethnic foods
36. Fast foods
37. Father's Day
38. Favorite ingredients
39. Fishing
40. Fourth of July
41. Freezer
42. Friendship
43. Fruit
44. Fruit punches

45. Garlic
46. Garden lovers
47. Going Away
48. Graduation
49. Grandchild
50. Grandparent
51. Gravy
52. Halloween
53. Herbs
54. Hiking snacks
55. Historical
56. Holiday
57. Ice Cream
58. Jams, jellies, marmalades, and preserves
59. Junk food
60. Love and romance
61. Low-fat / Fat-free
62. Lunch
63. Marinades
64. Meats
65. Microwave
66. Mother's Day
67. Muffins
68. No-cook
69. Party
70. Pastas
71. Pies and tarts
72. Picnic
73. Pot Luck
74. Reunion
75. Salads
76. Salsas
77. Sandwiches
78. Sauces
79. Seafood
80. Senior citizen's
81. Singles
82. Snacks
83. Soups
84. Sports tailgate parties
85. Spring
86. Summer
87. Sushi
88. Tea
89. Teenagers
90. Thanksgiving
91. Thank you
92. Travel / vacation
93. Valentine's Day
94. Vegetables
95. Vegetarian
96. Wedding
97. Weight loss
98. Welcome to the neighborhood
99. Wine
100. Winter
101. Yogurt

APPENDIX

STEP-BY-STEP CHECKLIST

Planning Your Keepsake

- ☐ Decide how you want to format your table of contents, and how much detail you want to include.

- ☐ Choose which, if any, optional cookbook parts you want to include.

- ☐ If you want to build an index, decide which items you want to list.

- ☐ Select a theme and tone for your keepsake.

- ☐ Develop a title.

- ☐ Choose a one-page or two-page format.

- ☐ Decide whether you'll include memories, photos, or graphic images with your recipes.

- ☐ Buy an album or binder (if unbound, buy page protectors also).

Recipes

- ☐ Collect all the recipes. If you're using recipes from other contributors, eliminate any duplicates and make corrections as necessary.

- ☐ Make copies of any antique recipes; carefully store the originals.

- ☐ Adapt and record any recipes you need to modify.

- ☐ Choose one format for all your recipes.

- ☐ If you *don't want* to include memories, photos, or other materials with your recipes, skip to "Putting It All Together."

- ☐ If you *do want* to include memories, photos, or other materials with your recipes, draft your recipes in the format you've chosen. Double-check and correct any errors.

- ☐ Check all the recipes for consistent use of abbreviations and terms.

- ☐ Sort the recipes into categories or sections. File each category or section of recipes in a separate folder, envelope, or page protector.

Memories

- ❏ Make any necessary corrections to the memories provided by other family members.

- ❏ Draft memories or stories for your recipes. Review and edit after a few days.

- ❏ Collect any quotations, song lyrics, poems, or other journaling you want to include.

- ❏ If you *don't want* to include photos, illustrations, or other images with your recipes, skip to "Putting It All Together."

- ❏ If you *do want* to include photos, illustrations, or other images, file each memory with its corresponding recipe in the folders, envelopes, or page protectors.

Photos, Illustrations and Other Visual Images

- ❏ Sort and select the photos you want to include in your keepsake.

- ❏ Draft and edit photo captions. If you postponed writing your memories until you selected your photos, draft and edit those memories now.

- ❏ Draft or trace illustrations.

- ❏ Collect stickers, clip art, or other instant images.

- ❏ File each photo, drawing, and image with its corresponding recipe.

Putting It All Together: Journals and Albums with Sewn-in Pages

- ❏ Group your cookbook materials by what you want to include on individual pages. If you want to include an index, draft a list of items from your grouped materials now.

- ❏ Draft your cover page.

- ❏ Draft your dedication page, section pages and appendix (optional).

- ❏ Draft your table of contents. Don't list page numbers yet.

- ❏ Put all your materials in the order you want them to appear in your cookbook. Estimate the number of pages you'll need in your journal or album.

- ❏ Transcribe your draft materials onto your journal or album pages. Create each page in order from the front to the back of the journal or album. If you're adding borders to the pages, do so *before* adding other materials.

- ❏ Number each page, beginning with the first section page or recipe page. Don't number the cover page, the title or dedication pages, or the table of contents.

❏ Record the appropriate page numbers to your table of contents. YOUR COOKBOOK IS NOW COMPLETE.

Putting It All Together: Albums and Binders with Loose Pages

❏ Select the background paper for your first page.

❏ Add a page border (optional).

❏ Position and write, type, draw, trace, or mount items to the background paper. If you're using page pockets, size each component to fit into the pockets.

❏ Assign a temporary number to each completed page; list recipe titles and other items on a temporary index (optional).

❏ Repeat the same steps to create each of your remaining recipe and memory pages.

Assemble and Add Finishing Touches: Albums and Binders with Loose Pages

❏ Put your completed pages in order.

❏ Create section pages (optional). Insert each section page *in front* of the corresponding section of recipe pages.

❏ Develop any appendix items (optional). Place them *behind* the other completed pages.

❏ Assign a final number to each page (optional). When you're satisfied with the order of your pages, change the temporary page numbers to final page numbers.

❏ Create the table of contents. Double-check the page numbers of all entries to ensure accuracy. Place it *in front* of all other completed pages.

❏ Create the index (optional). Make sure the page numbers listed are correct. Place the index *behind* the other pages.

❏ Create the title page and dedication page (optional). Insert them *in front* of your table of contents.

❏ Develop the cover page. Insert in pocket on album cover, or place *in front* of all the other completed pages.

❏ Insert each page into a page protector.

❏ Place all materials into album or binder.

SUMMARY OF RESOURCES

Many of the vendors listed offer a variety of materials and supplies. Call for catalogs.

Albums

Century Photo Products
(800) 767-0777
http://www.20thcenturydirect.com
Good selection of albums, including an "easel" design. Personalizes covers and spines.

Creative Memories
(800) 341-5275
http://www.creativememories.com
Top-notch scrapbook albums sold through a network of home representatives.

Exposures
(800) 222-4947
Impressive collection of quality albums.

Hallmark
(800) 425-5627
http://www.hallmark.com
Good selection of albums and page protectors.

Pioneer
(818) 882-2161
http://www.pioneerphotoalbums.com
Good selection of acid-free albums, photo corners, and other materials.

Recipes Shared Organization Kit
(800) 642-6762
Book of pre-designed cookbook pages with room for handwritten recipes and memories.

Books and Magazines

Alphabet Soup
by Wasatch Mt. Design
(801) 969-1808
Series of booklets full of lettering ideas and styles.

The Art of Writing Scrapbook Stories
by Janice T. Dixon, Ph.D.
(801) 486-3873
http://www.mt-olympus-press.com
25-page booklet with suggestions for writing stories about your child.

The Memory Triggering Book
by Bob Wendlinger
(888) 534-8989
http://www.triggers.com
Instructions and exercises for beginning and advanced writers to improve journaling.

Borders and Beyond Idea Book
by Toni Nelson and Beth Reames
http://www.scrapramento.com
Also available in scrapbook shops. 52 pages of ideas for creating page borders.

Creating Keepsakes Magazine
(888) 247-5298
http://www.creatingkeepsakes.com
Monthly scrapbooking magazine has lots of examples and ideas for page designs and information on helpful products and tools.

Memory Makers Magazine
(800) 366-6465
http://www.memorymakersmagazine.com
Monthly scrapbooking magazine has lots of examples and ideas for page designs and information on helpful products and tools.

Turning Memories Into Memoirs
by Denis Ledoux
Step-by-step instructions and exercises to write life stories. Available from retail and online bookstores.

Cookbook Publishers

All five of these publishers specialize in fundraising cookbooks and provide a variety of services, cookbook styles, and cover designs:

Cookbooks by Morris Press
(800) 445-6621
http://morriscookbooks.com

Cookbook Publishers, Inc.
(800) 227-7282
http://www.cookbookpublishers.com

G&R Publishing Company
(800) 383-1679
http://www.cookbookprinting.com

Gateway Publishing Co.
(800) 665-4878.
http://www.gatebook.com.

General Publishing & Binding, Inc.
(888) 397-0892.
http://www.fundraising-cookbooks.com

Tools

The Journaling Genie
Chatterbox
(208) 286-9517
http://www.chatterboxpub.com
Stencils help create handwritten journaling in a variety of shapes.

Decorative photo corners
Pebbles in My Pocket
(800) 438-8153
http://www.pebblesinmypocket.com
Full line of scrapbooking materials, including a variety of decorative photo corners.

Random Mount Protective Photo Holders
C. R. Gibson
Individual adhesive-backed photo protectors. Available in photo and scrapbooking stores.

un-du Adhesive Remover
Doumar Products, Inc.
(888) 289-8638
http://www.un-du.com
Safely removes photos adhered to album pages. Available in craft stores.

Adhesive background papers
SticSure
(714) 572-1213
8 1/2" x 11" sheets of acid-free, adhesive background papers in 16 different designs.

Internet Sites

Recipes and nutritional analysis

Cyber Kitchen
http://www.cyber-kitchen.com
Great site with links to many other cooking and food-related websites.

Digital Chef
http://www.digitalchef.com
Developed with the Culinary Institute of America, this site has recipes and much more.

The Kitchen Link
http://www.kitchenlink.com
Over 9,800 recipes and links to other cooking sites on the Internet.

Meals for You
http://www.mymenus.com
Lots of recipes, a good search engine, and many helpful questions and answers.

Recipes Online
http://recipes.wenzel.net
A robust database of 25,000 recipes and cooking information.

The Cook's Thesaurus
http://www.switcheroo.com
Thousands of ingredient definitions and substitutions.

Clip art, photos, and fonts

Arttoday
http://www.arttoday.com
Unlimited use of over 200,000 clip art images, fonts, and photos available for a minimal annual fee.

Software

ABC's of Creative Lettering
by Lindsay Ostrom
(916) 482-2288
http://www.scrapramento.com
An award-winning guide with simple and elaborate lettering.

Behind It All
by Homespun Software
(800) 727-2427
http://DSAmerica.com/homespun
Designs for creating your own background papers.

The Best of Creative Lettering
Creating Keepsakes Magazine
(888) 247-5282
http://www.creatingkeepsakes.com
This CD-ROM includes 12 different fonts and over 100 lettering designs.

Cook's Palate
by Better Lifestyles, Inc.
(888) 238-8377
http://www.cookspalate.com
Easy-to-use, well-designed software for creating, organizing, and printing cookbooks.

Creative Photo Albums Deluxe
by Dogbyte Development
(800) 936-4298
http://www.dogbyte.com
490 different page layouts and more than 30 different shapes for cropping photos.

Master Cook Deluxe
by Sierra-On-Line
(800) 617-7638
http://www.mastercook.com
Computerized expandable database containing 5,000 recipes, nutritional analysis, and a meal planner.

Photo Deluxe
Adobe Systems, Inc.
(800) 888-6293
http://www.adobe.com
Imaging software to import and edit photos: corrects color; contrast and sharpness; resizes; rotates; and crops.

Picture It!
Microsoft
(800) 426-9400
http://www.microsoft.com/pictureit
Easy-to-use imaging software to edit, resize, and crop photos.

Print Shop
by Broderbund
(800) 548-1798
http://www.printshop.com
Contains more than 100,000 graphics, images, and photos, and almost 6,600 different pre-designed page layouts. Also edits photos.

COOKING TERMS

Bake	Cook food in an oven.
Baste	Brush or spoon liquid over food while cooking to add flavor and moisturize.
Beat	Incorporating air into a mixture by stirring or mixing rapidly to make a fluffier, lighter mixture.
Blanch	Immerse food in boiling water, then immediately remove (usually to precook or loosen skin for easier peeling).
Blend	Thoroughly combine ingredients.
Boil	Heat liquid to a temperature of 212° F (bubbles form on the surface).
Braise	Cook food slowly in a small amount of liquid or fat in a covered pan on the stove or in the oven.
Bread	Coat with bread or cracker crumbs, flour, or cornmeal before cooking.
Broil	Cook in a gas or electric broiler.
Carmelize	Heat sugar or onions over low heat without scorching, until they turn golden brown and develop caramel-like color and flavor.
Clarify	Purify solid matter from stock or fats.
Combine	Mix together two or more ingredients.
Cream	Blend ingredients (usually butter and sugar) with spoon or electric mixer until smooth.
Cut in	Combine solid fat into dry ingredients (usually shortening into flour), using two knives or a pastry blender, until mixture resembles texture specified in recipe.
Deglaze	Make a sauce by adding liquid to cooking pan to dissolve bits of cooked meat, poultry, or fish stuck to the pan bottom.
Dice	Chop into small cubes.
Dredge	Coat food lightly with flour, sugar, or crumbs.

Drizzle   Sprinkle with drops of liquid.

Dust   Sprinkle food with dry ingredients, usually flour, cornmeal, or sugar.

Fold   Gently combine a light substance into a heavier mixture (whipped cream or beaten egg whites into batter, for example).

Fry   Cook in hot fat.

Glaze   Coat food with liquid during cooking to add shine or color.

Julienne   Cut food into matchstick-size slices.

Knead   Work a yeast dough with hands.

Mince   Chop finely.

Parboil   Partially cook by boiling.

Pare/Peel   Remove the skin of fruit or vegetables.

Pit   Remove the seed from whole fruits.

Poach   Cook in simmering (lightly boiling) liquid.

Preheat   Bring oven to the temperature specified in the recipe before putting in food.

Purée   Blend solid food into a thick mixture.

Reduce   Boil liquid until its volume is decreased (thickens liquid and concentrates flavor).

Roast   Bake uncovered and without liquids.

Sauté   Cook in a frying pan with a small amount of hot fat.

Scald   Heat milk just to the boiling point.

Score   Make shallow cuts on the surface of a food before baking.

Sear	Brown meat surfaces quickly over high heat.
Sift	Lighten dry ingredient(s) or remove lumps (usually flour) by forcing through a sifter.
Simmer	Cook very gently below the boiling point (bubbles barely break the surface of liquid).
Skim	Remove fat or film from the surface of food.
Steam	Cook food in vapors by placing it in a container or pan that is placed over a second container of boiling liquid.
Steep	Pour boiling liquid over food and allow it to sit.
Stew	Cook food slowly in a covered pot of simmering liquid.
Whip	Beat lightly to incorporate air and increase volume.
Whisk	Beat or whip with a whisk until blended and smooth.
Zest	Cut or scrape colored peel of citrus fruits.

STANDARD RECIPE ABBREVIATIONS

Measurement	Abbreviation*
cup	c.
teaspoon	t. or tsp.
tablespoon	T. or Tbsp.
ounce	oz.
pound	lb.
pint	pt.
quart	qt.
gallon	gal.

* Use the same abbreviations consistently throughout your cookbook.

Index

We'd love to hear from you!

Drop us a line, fax, or e-mail to share your comments, suggestions, and experiences regarding this book. We would also love to see a copy of your recipe and memory pages. If we use your suggestions or photos in our next publication, we'll say thank you with a 25% discount on the book's cover price. (Sorry, we cannot return photos.)

- I am: ❑ Female   ❑ Male

- How did you receive our book?

    ❑ Purchased   ❑ Received as a gift   ❑ Other _____

- What I liked best about the book was: ❑ Examples   ❑ Do It Yourself checklists

    ❑ Tips 'n Tools   ❑ Other_____

- I'd like the book better if:_____

    _____

- Please describe any helpful tips or techniques you discovered while creating your keepsake cookbook (attach additional pages if needed).

    _____

    _____

- I'm enclosing a photo of one of my keepsake cookbook pages.

    ❑ You may use it in your future publications   ❑ Do not publish my photo(s)

_____   _____
[Signature authorizing use]   [date]

Please print the following (or just attach your return address label)

_____

[Name]

_____
{Street Address/PO Box]   [City]   [State] [Zip]

(_____)_____
[Telephone No.]   [Best time to contact if necessary]   [E-mail address]

E-mail: to: carlop@pacbell.net
Fax: (650) 592-3790
Mail: Carlo Press   P.O. Box 7080   San Carlos, CA 94070-7080

ORDER FORM

Mail Orders: Carlo Press, PO Box 7080, San Carlos, CA 94070

Toll-Free: (800) 431-1579

Fax Orders: (650) 592-3790

On the Internet: www.carlopress.com or www.amazon.com

E-mail: carlop@pacbell.net

Please send me _____ copies x $18.95 each = $_____

       CA residents add $1.56 tax for each book $_____

       Shipping: $3.20 $_____
       (Free shipping for 3 or more books)

       Total $_____

☐ Check

☐ Credit Card: ___VISA   ___Mastercard   ___American Express   ___Discover

Card number:_____

Name on card:_____Exp. date:_____

Ship to:_____

       _____

Tel: _____

This is a gift. Send directly to: ☐ Please autograph

Name:_____

Address:_____

We'll gladly refund 100% of the cover price if you are not completely satisfied.